The
Sociological
Task

The
Sociological
Task

Harold Fallding

University of Waterloo, Ontario

PRENTICE-HALL, INC.
Englewood Cliffs, New Jersey

Prentice-Hall Sociology Series
Neil J. Smelser, *Editor*

The author gratefully acknowledges the kind permission of the publisher
to reprint the quotation that appears on the opposite page: George C.
Homans, *The Human Group* (London: Routledge & Kegan Paul Ltd., 1951),
p. 22.

Library of Congress Catalog Card No.: 68–24428

Current printing (*last number*):

10 9 8 7 6 5 4 3

Printed in the United States of America

PRENTICE-HALL INTERNATIONAL, INC., *London*
PRENTICE-HALL OF AUSTRALIA, PTY. LTD., *Sydney*
PRENTICE-HALL OF CANADA, LTD., *Toronto*
PRENTICE-HALL OF INDIA PRIVATE LTD., *New Delhi*
PRENTICE-HALL OF JAPAN, INC., *Tokyo*

Let us make the important quantitative,
and not the quantitative important.

George C. Homans, *The Human Group*

Preface

Over a period of years now, the writing of this book has been my real vocation, even though the business of my occupation has lain in a host of other things. It has had a prolonged and agonizing delivery. It is not a long book, but there was never an extended period when I could work at it with undivided attention. A person such as I am, whose mind is in a fever until its ideas are expressed, could well do with the customary sabbatical year. But in the twelve years of university teaching and research that have followed my doctoral studies at the Australian National University, I have not been able to enjoy that respite. Nor would I normally expect to do so now for four or five years to come. Starting at a great disadvantage in Australia, where opportunities for scholarly work in sociology were next to nonexistent, I have followed each hope of better opportunity. The long summer of the Canadian academic year has, at length, made it possible for me to bring the book to completion. A research grant from the Canada Council during the summer of 1967 and summer research fellowships from the university itself during that and the summer preceding, provided material support. The torrid struggle for the conditions of creative work that writing this book represents, leaves me utterly convinced that universities should remain places apart for the pursuit of scholarship. There has been much talk about academicians becoming involved in the community in order to apply their knowledge. Let those who are called to it apply knowledge. Others of us are called to seek it out, and that is a public service in its own right and one that requires a certain sequestering.

Because its birth was protracted in the way I have described, part of this book appeared first in what might almost be called installments. The outline of the argument was drawn in three journal articles issued at different times (1962, 1963, and 1966) on three continents (Australia, the United States, and Norway). With certain revisions, these articles are reproduced as part of the text of the book. Acknowledgment is given to the Editors concerned for permission to reproduce "The Scope and Purpose of Sociology," *Australian Journal of Politics and History*, 3:1 (1962), 78–92, which makes part of Chapter 5; "Functional Analysis in Sociology," *American Sociological Review*, 28 (1963), 5–13, which has been used in Chapters 6 and 8; and "Ideology and the Functional Analysis of Cultures," *Inquiry*, 9 (1966), 241–61, which has been used in Chapters 6 and 7. In addition, a small section of a fourth paper is reproduced. Some paragraphs on community in Chapter 8, 106–8, are reprinted by permission from the *Quarterly Journal of Studies on Alcohol*, 25 (1964), 714–24 (Copyright by *Journal of Studies on Alcohol Inc.*, New Brunswick, N.J.).

Should this book be read by students of my graduate seminars at Rutgers, The State University, New Jersey, and at the University of Waterloo, it will seem very familiar. It was battered into shape in the course of discussions with them. My debt to certain of these students is greater than I can ever say. For there is no more necessary stimulus for a professor, nor any greater reward, than the response of awakened minds.

The typing of the manuscript and its drafts was the work of Mrs. M. Thomson, secretary of our Department of Sociology and Anthropology in the University of Waterloo. Mrs. Thomson's work was exquisitely and faithfully executed, and it was also done with intelligent understanding and complete identification.

HAROLD FALLDING

Contents

part 2
Empirical Measurement
by Evaluation
of Function

The
Sociological
Task

Introduction

This book expresses the conviction that sociology is a science with a future and that what it is waiting for now is measurement—moreover, that measurement *of what* is important by itself. Sociologists have been accused of measuring what is measurable in place of measuring what matters. It would be a pity if the element of truth in this accusation left anyone antipathetic to measurement in general. Measurement does not imply triviality of itself: without it we cannot know variation. Conversely, where we claim to see variation we are measuring, however crudely. What we call "events" are any perceptible quantitative changes. If something appears where it did not appear before we have at the very least measured from zero to unity—more commonly we claim to see new things "grow." If we think that cases vary in such ways as a party growing rowdier, a prejudice deeper, a friendship closer, a government shakier, or a clique more influential, we are measuring.

An explanatory science establishes principles by finding that one thing may be expected to vary with another. So whenever we entertain an explanation, measurements will be at hand for more things than one. We see that the party grows rowdier as more liquor is swallowed, that prejudice hardens as misunderstandings persist longer, that a friendship is cemented as exchanged favors multiply.

The item in the pair occurring first in time can be accepted as the explanation of the later one. But, in addition, we may wish to have the co-variations themselves explained. And explained they are by showing that, on other occasions, each item of the pair has separately been found to vary with yet a third item, this third item occurring after

1

one of them in time but before the other. People talk more when their conventional restraints have been reduced, and their conventional restraints are progressively reduced as they consume more alcohol. The longer misconceptions persist the more social distance widens, and the more social distance widens the more does prejudice harden. And so on.

Indeed, there need be no end to the proliferation of these explanatory third factors, budding in the fork of factors already paired. For every third factor can itself become a member of two pairs, each of which can beget its own third factor in turn. In this way a body of connected explanations is filled in like thickening spokes in a wheel. The form of advancing theory, then, is that of a radiating, centrally budding bush. Each branch in it represents a distinct dimension of measurement. These hang together in pairs, made up of what we take to be caused and causing factors.

The purpose of this book is not to say *how* sociological measurements may be made but to say *what* should be measured if measurements are to be sociological. The preoccupation with dimensions of measurement does not reflect a concern with technique so much as with systematization. This, surely, is the prior consideration. Techniques will have to be worked out in the end, but there is a certain futility in elaborating techniques until we know what things are relevant to our inquiry. *What* to measure in sociology, not *how* to measure, is to be our theme.

The book divides into two parts, and it is in the second part that the actual dimensions of sociological measurement are set down, in Chapters 7 and 8 specifically. Chapter 9 illustrates the general applicability of the dimensions to groups of all sizes. The concluding and tenth chapter points out some of the implications for method of the view of the social process advanced.

It seems that the champion of a science of society is still obliged to show wherein the distinctiveness of social facts lies; this is attempted in the chapter with which Part II opens, Chapter 5. Then in Chapter 6 it is argued that, because we are considering systems in sociology, an evaluation of their functioning is inherent in our account of them and that this evaluation is in fact our measurement. Thus we are led to find our dimensions of measurement in what have been called *functional imperatives* or *system states*. Yet functionalism is embraced in such a way as to make the dialectical and evolutionary accounts of society complementary to it. Simultaneously, *social pathology* acquires a generic meaning as any dysfunctional state.

The four chapters of Part I are designed to show the necessity for such a model of the social process as Part II sets forth; for there has been a great deal of confusion over what "theory" is in sociology. A major source of the confusion has been the failure to distinguish *explanatory theory* from what might be called *analytical theory*, which is quite different: the role of the latter is heuristic, not explanatory. Part I shows that both kinds of "theory" are necessary, the only profitable course for the sociological enterprise being to pass from analytical to explanatory theory by making empirical measurement. I insist that a certain subtlety and system are needed for this. The terms of scientific discussion can differ in their nature, so we need to know these different vehicles in the mind and the kind of load they can carry.

part **I**

The Only Profitable Course:
from Conceptual Scheme
to Explanatory Theory
via Empirical Measurement

chapter 1

Explanation as the Pairing
of Variables

Lazarsfeld has called a third factor introduced to clarify the relationship between two others a *test factor*.[1] We test the significance of that relationship by testing whether this third, test factor intervenes in time between them. If we establish that it does, we have a case of what Lazarsfeld chooses to call *interpretation* rather than *explanation*. He reserves the term *explanation* for the simpler situation in which we satisfy ourselves that the first of two variables causes the second. But he claims that we only do this if we can allay all suspicion that the first is in association with the second because of the influence of a hitherto unexamined factor which occurs still earlier in time. (A hitherto unexamined factor would become the test factor in this instance.) I am not persuaded, however, that we require a factor to be a pure original in this way to accept it as a cause. For one thing, the task of eliminating possible earlier causes becomes impossible, for we have no way of knowing when we are through. According to Lazarsfeld, if the presumed cause operates independently it is "real"; if it is caused to seem a cause it is "spurious." But I believe we should accept as a cause any factor which varies with and before a second one, provided we can ascribe a fitness to the conjunction. Lazarsfeld uses two illustrations to show what he means by a "spurious cause": Birthrates increase as the incidence of storks in the area increases; and the damage caused by a fire increases in proportion to the number of fire engines fighting it. He says we would be wrong

---

[1] P. F. Lazarsfeld and M. Rosenberg, eds., *The Language of Social Research, A Reader in the Methodology of Social Research* (New York: The Free Press of Glencoe, Inc., 1955), pp. 115–25.

to take the incidence of storks and number of fire engines as causing the birth rate and extent of damage. It is really rural environment that causes the higher birthrate, and the size of the fire the amount of damage. These also separately cause the incidence of storks and number of engines. But I find myself compelled to ask why we would stop at that, or how we would know that these rather than others are the real causes. It could be argued that it is not really the rural environment but rural subculture that influences birthrate. Similarly, one could object that it is not really the area under flames that determines the amount of damage but the value of the property destroyed. I cannot believe there is any elimination procedure that can establish one cause as true.

Lazarsfeld takes *interpretation* and *explanation* for two types of *elaboration*, a third being *specification*. Specification comes into play when the relation between two variables is altered as a third factor is altered. It contrasts with interpretation, where the constancy of the relation between two variables is a function of the alteration of the third and more or less guaranteed by it. Specification is a matter of specifying the conditions under which *different* relationships between the first pair of variables hold: their relationship is different for different values of the third variable. It is essentially a matter of mentally resorting the world into artificial subworlds—strata—in each of which the cases are uniform for the third variable. Consider a case from Berelson, Lazarsfeld and McPhee's study *Voting*.[2] At first it seems surprising that in Elmira, N.Y., persons of both high and low socio-economic status are predominantly Republican in their party preference. But closer scrutiny shows this is only the case if nonmembership in unions is high among the sample studied. If union members are considered separately, a Democratic party preference predominates among low-status persons and the two preferences are equal in the case of high-status persons. Nonmembership in unions is thus the condition under which the original relationship holds, and Lazarsfeld is therefore inclined to call the relation a *conditional relation*. There is another case in Lazarsfeld and Thielens' study *The Academic Mind*.[3] Colleges were classified by the amount of pressure politicians brought to bear on them and the support the administration gave to faculty. There seemed to be scarcely any relation between the two. But this random picture was not sustained when the sample was divided into two subsamples of state and private colleges. In state universities there was a tendency for administrators

[2] B. R. Berelson, P. F. Lazarsfeld, and W. M. McPhee, *Voting, A Study of Opinion Formation in a Presidential Campaign* (Chicago: The University of Chicago Press, 1954), pp. 37–53.

[3] P. F. Lazarsfeld and W. Thielens, Jr., *The Academic Mind: Social Scientists in a Time of Crisis* (New York: The Free Press of Glencoe, Inc., 1958), pp. 159–91.

both to yield to political pressure and to withdraw protection from faculty. In private institutions the tendency was to resist and even counteract the political pressure and to support the faculty. A third illustration of specification may be taken from Pelz's study of research performance.[4] It was found that if scientists were given a great deal of freedom to make their own work decisions by their directors, their productivity was greater—the closer the consulting contacts the director maintained with them. The qualifying rider indicates the limiting condition, the stratum or subsample, for which the relationship is true. That is, unless the research workers were kept in close consultation with the director, greater freedom did not mean greater output. It is pedantic to make specification a necessary step in research, as some seem to want to do. It is an optional step, of course, and we only need to make it if the artificial strata correspond to realities about which we have questions to ask. But, again, this comes down to considering factors in pairs, the relationship between the first pair of variables becoming a factor in its own right in this instance.

It appears that in all analytical or scientific thinking (certainly in these varieties of what Lazarsfeld calls "elaboration") we are effecting a drastic simplification by turning our attention from the multiplicity of things to two. These two things we seek to connect by verbal definition and/or mathematical equation and pass thence, by a web of interconnections, to a coherent account of the world. The connections and web are made when the same terms are linked with different mates in different definitions or equations. The point of considering more than two factors is quite misunderstood unless it is seen as a pathway that returns us to simplicity in examining pair relationships. It is both mistaken and unnecessary to hope that such multivariate analysis holds some promise of instantaneously picturing the complex world in its rich complexity. We all know the world is complex and do not want to have to name everything in it on one breath: we want to know what pairs of things give it order by being related.

There is a special problem which it is often hoped multivariate analysis can help solve. This is to tell us what fraction of the variance of a factor is to be accounted for by each of several others that have some causal influence on it. It has been asked, for instance, whether raising people's economic status is more important than reducing immigration in coping with juvenile delinquency. One may agree with Stouffer that this is a legitimate question for a sociologist to ask.[5] But such

4 D. C. Pelz, "Some Social Factors Related to Performance in a Research Organization," *Administrative Science Quarterly*, 1 (1956), 310–25.

5 S. A. Stouffer, *Social Research to Test Ideas* (New York: The Free Press of Glencoe, Inc., 1962), pp. 261–73.

questions are only answerable if the causal factors are all convertible
to specifiable degrees of one factor—of some generalized thing like force,
energy, mass, weight, or strain. In the instance referred to, we would
need to be able to convert measures of economic status and of the
foreign-born population into some common term—such as "disadvantage," for instance—so that the question can again be posed in terms
of a meaningful relationship between a pair of factors.

I cannot acquiesce in the practice of measuring the relative strengths
of two causal factors by the incidence of the same caused result in samples
where each of them operates alone. Durkheim found a lower suicide
rate among widowers with children than among married men who are
childless.[6] What are we entitled to conclude from this? We can hardly
conclude that the parental tie gives greater immunity to suicide than
the marital bond. To say that one factor effects a certain result in
more cases when it operates alone is not to say it would do it more
strongly in cases where the factors operate in combination. We must
recognize that it can be the resultant of multiple factors that determines
the immunity exhibited in each individual sample. It is significant that
suicide occurs at all in either sample. That it occurs less frequently in one
than the other simply poses larger questions. What are all the factors that
can operate to inhibit it? Are their measures convertible?

The tendency toward simplification of the complex world is more
directly evident in factor analysis, yet even here it is not always appreciated that the relationship of pairs is our ultimate goal. For in factor
analysis all we are doing is accounting for the pair-relationships among
a group of variables by the pair-relationships among a smaller group.
Our concern is scarcely to explain at all, but to describe data more
succinctly: it is essentially a summarizing operation. As often as not,
factor analysis is little more than a compensation for conceptual poverty
or clumsiness, the science not having generated significant concepts which
could cut across common-sense items. As likely as not, nothing is finally
added to explanatory theory, inasmuch as the factors can be without
definition or name. Bell compared census tracts in the San Francisco
Bay region according to seven different indices, viz., scores for occupation, education, rent, fertility, women in the labor force, single-family
dwelling units, and the relative number of persons in subordinate
ethnic groups.[7] The correlation of each index with the others gave a
matrix from which three factors were extracted. Two of the factors
correlated highly with certain indices, but these were so miscellaneous

6 E. Durkheim, *Suicide, A Study in Sociology,* trans. A. Spaulding and G. Simpson,
ed. G. Simpson (London: Routledge & Kegan Paul, Ltd., 1952), pp. 171–216.

7 W. Bell, "Economic, Family, and Ethnic Status: An Empirical Test," *American
Sociological Review,* **20** (1955), 45–52.

as to give no clue to the meaning of the factors. Thus a new set of three different factors was extracted. Each of these was so correlated with a selection of the indices as to seem meaningful, so they were named. A factor correlating highly with the first three of the listed indices was named "economic status," one correlating with the next three was named "family status," one correlating with the seventh was named "ethnic status."

No. There is nothing in any *empirical method* which can take an instantaneous imprint of the rich complexity of the world. *This is wholly the gift to us of the comprehensiveness and coherence of propositional theory.* All empirical methods are analytical, instruments of dissection.

Diagram 1 shows how the rudimentary pair-pattern, represented by a vee, is at the heart of each of Lazarsfeld's types of elaboration. Each

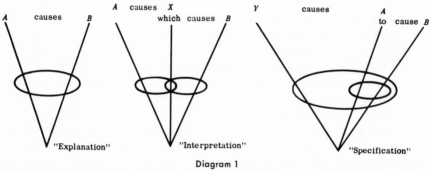

Diagram 1

distinct pair is looped with a ring. Throughout this book, the term *explanation* will be used with this general meaning. It will refer essentially to a pair-relationship in which variation in the first factor of a pair is said to be a cause of the variation of the second. Thus defined, it is part of all three of Lazarsfeld's types of elaboration.

In seemingly more complicated varieties of explanation the explanatory element is still the same. We may take, for example, the five "methods" of explanation examined by Robert Brown:[8] (1) genetic, (2) intentions, (3) dispositions, (4) reasons, and (5) functions. If we explain some event genetically we give an account of the sequence of events leading up to it. But if that ever seems to make a plausible explanation, it is only because the more anterior event of each pair in the sequence can be accepted as causing the succeeding one. The injustice built into a constitution may generate a chain of events that culminates in rebellion, for instance. Also, if we accept someone's intention as the explanation of his action, it is only because we can be-

[8] R. Brown, *Explanation in Social Science* (Chicago: Aldine Publishing Co., 1963).

lieve that his intention successfully triggered a chain of events that produced the action. A politician may reverse the previous vote in his electorate because, entirely as a result of his intention, the reputation of his opponent has been damaged. It is the same with dispositions. We are prepared to impute causally effective force to a disposition just as we do to an intention, provided nothing keeps it from having the effect we have learned to expect. A person may continually refuse nomination for office because he has a disposition to shyness and consequently remains unknown to the public. The situation is similar again for reasons. To explain an event in terms of the reason a person had for bringing it about is to imply that he was successful in accomplishing something he desired. His having a reason was a causally effective factor in the chain of events. A person may sell his shares on the stock market for the reason that he wants to realize fluid capital. Finally, there is the attempt to "explain" an event by stating its function. Here we encounter something a little different. Yet the difference simply consists in the fact that we invert our mode of expression. For if we are explaining anything at all by stating a function, we are using the event itself to explain its effects. Nagel has demonstrated this.[9] For instance, if we say that two functions of the family are procreation and socialization, all we mean, so far as explanation is concerned, is that procreation and socialization are results of the way people cooperate in families.

Although I have considered it important to deny that multivariate analysis comes to anything more in the end than the analysis of factors in pairs, I recognize that it has special advantages. Possibly the most important has to do with the factor that is stratified. If any factor *can* be stratified in this way it is a pretty potent force in the world, *and it is factors of this kind that explanatory sciences are in urgent pursuit of.* For these, it will be remembered, are factors which control the relationships of other factors. They exert a causal influence that is, so to speak, raised to a higher power. If we can isolate factors which control the relatonships of other factors, we are moving toward the basic dimensions of our science.

This has been grasped readily enough in the empirical work of many sociologists. It has been realized, for instance, that the influence of a factor might vary radically between societies. So a cross-cultural sample has been taken. It has been realized that, within a society, the basic and pervasive likenesses that generate "community" will differentiate within the population. So the data are stratified for race, nationality, religion, urban or rural settlement, social class, occupation. It is realized that the allocation of roles within a society is largely dictated

9 E. Nagel, "A Formalization of Functionalism," in *Logic Without Metaphysics* (New York: The Free Press of Glencoe, Inc., 1956), pp. 247–83.

by age and sex, ability and training, so the data are stratified along these dimensions. Yet, although all this gives evidence of an awareness of fruitful procedure, it does not yet show a great deal of conceptual aptitude in slicing up society by the dimensions inherent in it as a dynamic process. As I have said, it is the purpose of this book to make suggestions as to what these dimensions might be.

chapter 2

The Nonempirical Intervening Variable
as the Connecting Link of Explanation

I have shown that *explanation* is taking the variation in the first factor of a pair to be a cause of the variation of the second. This is the bare bones of the matter. It can be more complex; yet when it is, it is made up of this as the element. It has also been pointed out that the relationship between one factor and an antecedent explaining factor can be viewed as a single thing and itself explained. We have the feeling, then, that our "explanation" is being "explained." There is nothing surprising about this regression, which can be continuing. But we should give attention to that particular case where the final explaining factor is not empirically observable but an entire fiction, an image of the mind. This is frequently called the *hypothetical*, or *theoretical*, *construct*: an atom, a force, a motive, for instance. Some keep the term *intervening variable* exclusively for these constructs, and I shall follow this practice, for it seems useful. If we adopt this convention, however, and designate only the nonempirical variable as "intervening," we should *not* use that term for the third factor in Lazarsfeld's *interpretation*. Nadel is one author to use the term in the way I do here, and he refers to a similar use of it by Poincaré, Lewin, Tolman, and Cohen.[1] Lazarsfeld has a

1 S. F. Nadel, *The Foundations of Social Anthropology* (London: Cohen & West, 1951), pp. 191–221; H. Poincaré, *The Value of Science* (New York: Dover Publications, Inc., 1958), pp. 112–28; K. Lewin, *The Conceptual Representation and the Measurement of Psychological Forces* (Durham, N.C.: Duke University Press), 1938, pp. 11–19; E. C. Tolman, "Physiology, Psychology and Sociology," *Psychological Review*, 45 (1938), 228–41; M. R. Cohen, *A Preface to Logic* (London: Routledge & Kegan Paul, Ltd., 1946), pp. 71–2.

notion of his own that seems to be virtually identical, which he calls
the *classificatory concept*.[2]

It is not necessary that every quest for explanation be pushed to
this nonempirical limit. But if it is, we seem to gain two advantages.
It is, first of all, a final plug in the breach in our understanding, a final
rest to our feverish questioning. To invent entities like this is to say
Amen. Here we come to the limit of the regression of explanations. For
theoretical entities, although serving to explain empirical ones, do not
themselves beg to be explained: it might almost be said they beg
off explanation. They line the mind with velvet and make us feel at
home in the world. Yet it would be wrong to say that grasping at such
comfort is contrary to the spirit of science. For our intention in seeking
for explanation is to secure that comfort. Nor are theoretical entities
a block to further empirical inquiry: we only use or tolerate them
when we have exhausted the power of experience to answer our questions.

But more important than being psychologically satisfying, these
fictions have the advantage of bridge-building and, by virtue of the
bridges built, of opening up the closed thoroughfares of our mind into
circuits for a continuous traffic of knowledge. By this figure I refer only
partly to the well-known generalizing property of theoretical concepts.
Because it is abstract, any such concept can accommodate a whole range
(a class) of concrete instances. But, over and above this, by it we may
pass across the gap between seemingly disparate classes of empirical
facts. For every such concept is so invented as to have a fitness with
not one but two classes of phenomena, and possibly with more than
two. If we were to use another metaphor, we might liken the nonempirical intervening variable to a joint in a building set which slips
onto two or more differently shaped parts. It has one main stem that
matches one part of the set, one or more branching arms that match
other different parts. By using such joints, a whole collection of disparate parts can be linked in one. It is thus that our picture of the world
gets coherence. It does so by the process we have recognized, of linking
things in simple pairs. For, if the concept is a joint with more than
one branching arm, it will comprise a set of pairs: one branch and the
stem in each case. But all this needs illustration.

Let us think first of Poincaré's example from physics. If we say
that heavy bodies falling freely pass over spaces that are proportional
to the squares of the times, we are, Poincaré says, simply giving the
definition of free fall. From our point of view it is important that
this definition incorporates two variables: increasing time of fall in

2 From "Problems in Methodology" by Paul F. Lazarsfeld, in *Sociology Today*,
edited by R. K. Merton, L. Broom, and L. S. Cottrell, Jr., © 1959 by Basic Books, Inc.,
Publishers, New York.

space is associated with increasing velocity of travel. We may leave it at that or we may seek to pass behind it and explain it. In the latter case we introduce the fictitious entity "gravitation." An increasing time of fall leads to the body being exposed to an increasing time of application of a force, "gravity," and this leads to an increasing velocity of travel. Diagram 2 illustrates how the concept of gravity *intervenes* in the explanatory sequence.

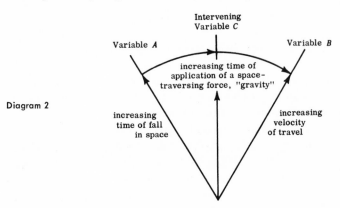

Diagram 2

Notice the way in which the intervening variable has a fitness with both of the variables it is wedged between. The space-traversing force fits with free fall in space. Force is known to produce acceleration, so it fits with increase in velocity.

As a second illustration, we may consider the concept of "intelligence." This is a concept to which Lewin makes reference in his discussion of the intervening variable. Our first observation is that different people differ not only in their capacity to see any one relationship, but persons who are more astute in seeing one relationship tend to be more astute in seeing another. Again, we may leave it at that or we may seek to explain it. In the latter case, we introduce the fictitious entity "intelligence," which we define as some kind of ability to perceive relationships. Diagram 3 illustrates how this concept intervenes in the explanatory sequence.

Notice again the way in which the intervening variable has a fitness with the variables on either side of it. An ability is part of the makeup we attribute to persons. A generalized ability to repeat achievements of the same kind fits with the consistency the person demonstrates in performance.

I have said that Lazarsfeld's notion of a *classificatory concept* is virtually identical with the nonempirical intervening variable of other authors. In one of his more recent papers he examines its nature.[3] More

3 *Ibid.*

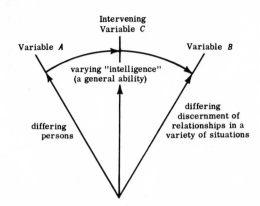

Diagram 3

than anyone else, he succeeds in showing how it makes a two- or multi-sided thing. Lazarsfeld says that we attribute to such concepts two distinct kinds of indicators: he calls them *expressive* and *predictive*. The expressive indicators make a fairly stable, central collection and express the concept in its most general aspect. The predictive indicators comprise a distinct subset (or there may be several subsets) which expresses that facet of the concept which is closest to the empirical variable it is invoked to explain. If the nonempirical intervening variable is used on different occasions to explain different variables, there may be a separate subset of predictive indicators for each occasion. In our metaphor, the expressive indicators comprise the stem and the predictive indicators the branch or branches of the joint. A consideration of two of Lazarsfeld's examples will make his meaning plainer.

He takes as a psychological example the authoritarian personality. First it was observed that different people exhibited different degrees of anti-Semitism. To explain the connection, a very generalized personality trait, *authoritarianism*, was postulated, which came to be measured by the original F-scale. Some of the indicators in this concept were very general expressions of a person's willingness to have outside agencies make his moral decisions for him and also of his need to have trouble-generating impulses repressed. These were the expressive indicators. But there were other indicators that were quite close to anti-Semitism, more direct evidences of suspicion, prejudice, and hostility, and these were the predictive indicators. Lazarsfeld says that on other occasions, to explain other behavior by authoritarianism, different predictive indicators might be added that would go more specifically with it. The same notion had been current in the University of Frankfurt around 1930, where sociologists observed that certain German workers were more prone than others to acquiesce to the Hitler movement. They made a survey, using a questionnaire. Some items in this were very like the expressive indicators in the F-scale. But there were other predictive indicators that were "as closely related to the issues of the times as they could be without explicitly referring to the political Nazi programme." [4] Diagrams 4 and 5 show how the same intervening variable has

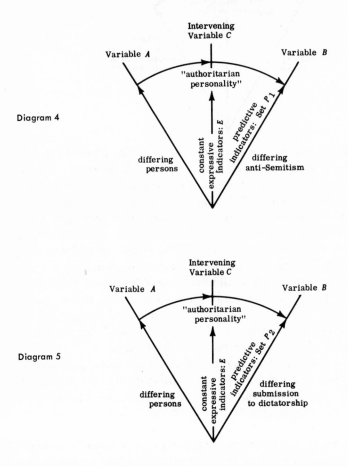

Diagram 4

Diagram 5

been used to explain two separated phenomena: anti-Semitism and submission to dictatorship. Then Diagram 6 shows how the concept of authoritarianism, so far as we have taken it here, can be viewed as a joint with one stem and two branching arms. By it, through a succession of simple pairs, seven separate elements of our thought and experience are knit into a unity. There is a gain in coherence in our picture of the world. And with each new set of predictive indicators, three more elements are grafted to the tree.

[4] *Ibid.,* p. 54.

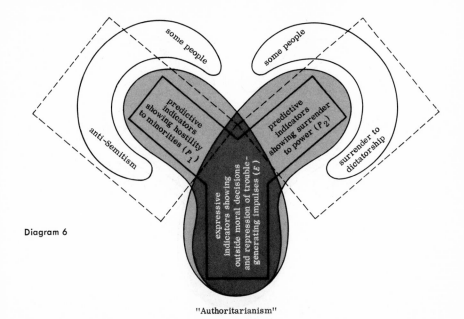

Diagram 6

"Authoritarianism"

As an instance of a sociological intervening variable Lazarsfeld considers Durkheim's notion of social integration. This reappears, Lazarsfeld believes, in American group dynamics as group cohesion. Originally developed to explain immunity to suicide, it had predictive indicators relevant to that phenomenon as well as expressive indicators that were more general. The predictive indicators had to do with the moderation of desires through internalization of norms and with freedom from anxiety through viewing oneself as the instrument of a greater purpose. The expressive indicators of integration had to do with the frequency and closeness of contact among the members of the group and with their moral consensus. Some recent workers in group dynamics have settled on the resistance of a group to breakup as being somehow related to integration. Now, Lazarsfeld claims that insofar as researchers introduce indicators to show this, they are adding another set of predictive indicators to integration, thereby grafting another branch to the stem. Diagram 7 shows how, once again, all this links seven elements of our thought and experience into one.

Some readers might question whether Lazarsfeld's "classificatory concepts" can be considered nonempirical variables at all, for they have empirical indicators. I choose to consider them such, if for no other reason than because the connection between indicator and thing indicated is made *by fiat*. The indicators strung together are, separately, empirical, but the assumption that they cohere and indicate something

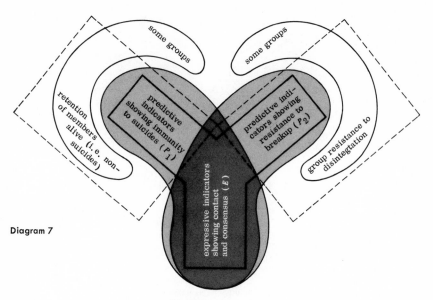

Diagram 7

"Social Integration"

beyond themselves is not. The nonempirical nature of the concepts therefore remains. As a matter of fact, the whole enterprise in science to operationalize concepts by indicators reveals an abiding faith in the nonempirical. It involves a frank recognition that scientific thought has both empirical and nonempirical elements. It seems important, however, also to recognize that whatever connection is believed to exist between the two can only be what is postulated. There can be no proof of it and we cannot get any more out of this procedure than we put into it.

It is generally recognized that explanation may be offered with or without benefit of an explicit nonempirical variable. It is also recognized that explanation in either form may be offered for a single recurring event or for a set of recurring events. What is called the *empirical generalization* or *experimental law* is the lowliest creature in the kingdom of explanation. It is the explanation of a single recurring event that does not invoke the nonempirical variable. The *theoretical law* is the explanation of this same event that does. The explanation schema explains a set of recurring events without invoking nonempirical variables. The deductive theory is the explanation of a set of events that does. The deductive theory is sovereign in the kingdom of explanation. In developing it, we aim to explain as many empirical generalizations and theoretical laws of the science as possible by the smallest possible set of assumptions, these assumptions including reference to unobservable entities.

Even though "explanation" is sometimes said to exist in a variety of kinds, I consider it to have only the *one form*, as I have indicated. Change in one variable (which may itself be the relationship between others) is seen to be associated with change in an antecedent one, and this antecedent one may be empirically knowable or purely an invention so far as accessibility to observation goes. I would argue further that we do not accept an explanatory factor as a "real," "true," or "plausible" explanation simply because it is invariably associated with another one, nor yet because we have eliminated other possible factors as spurious. We do so because, known to be invariably associated, it *seems to have some fitness* to what it is taken to explain. We impute this fitness if we can imagine something in between, having two faces, each of which has some analogical resemblance to the factor facing it. As I said, then, all explanations need not be pushed through to fictional, theoretical concepts intervening in an explicit way; yet whenever we seriously consider whether we can accept an explanation as true or plausible, such concepts are at least implicitly involved. They seem to be *always* present, either in substance or shadow, in serious science. This is one of the reasons it is true to say that imagination is the heart of science and generating theory—plausible, not fantastic, theory—the greatest scientific gift.

I am not unaware that the wisdom of continuing with the whole notion of cause has been challenged. I continue to advocate it because I believe the motivation for inquiry springs from the conviction that causes can be known. If we cloak our searching in some more evasive form of words, it is this conviction that continues to motivate the search. Furthermore, we need not be worried by the fact that what we often find, or even learn in time to seek, are simply probabilities of connection between variables. The form of the thing is not different, and when I have referred to invariable association I have meant it as a shorthand that would include this case. For we impute a necessary causality here just the same, but make the mental reservation that the precise conditions within which it operates are not yet fully known.

At the close of the first chapter I said we would be aiming to identify explanatory factors of wide influence. We can now see how the search for them may lead us to nonempirical variables. To invoke such variables for explanation, however, means that we claim to have evidence that in some cases they are present and in others absent, or that when present they are present in variable degree. This means that at some point they will have been tied to empirical indicators. This may be done by a dovetail definition that slides the imaginary entity into an empirical groove, as *gravity* slides between an observed duration of fall and an observed increase of velocity of fall. Or it may be done by a pincushion definition, as *social integration* is studded with splinters of internalized norms and frequent and close social contact, etc. In both cases, variations in the world of experience are being accounted for by assumed variations somewhere behind it. But what is of equal importance is that these shadowy entities are each given an *operational definition,* as it has been called. We only assume them to vary insofar as there are observable variations at hand. Herein lies a great difference between the nonempirical explanatory concept and the nonempirical heuristic concept. They should not be taken for the same. The precise place of the nonempirical heuristic is something we shall turn to in the next chapter. Meanwhile, let us take note that the terms of explanation always have an empirical anchorage to some degree, even the nonempirical intervening variable. We do need a term, however, and in this book especially, to refer to concepts regardless of whether they are at the heuristic or explanatory stage of maturity, and for this we shall use the term *dimension.*

Two observations should be added before concluding this chapter. The first is that we should beware of an ever-present temptation, when we introduce intervening variables, to move into reductionist explanation. There is the idea that we are giving a deeper or more fundamental explanation of phenomena if we not only go behind them but if we go beneath the whole level of phenomena to which they belong. Specifically, in the case of sociological phenomena, this means attempting to explain them by going into "the psychology of it." There is even a feeling on the part of some that a concern with explanation in sociology is tantamount to an attachment to social psychology, inasmuch as social processes are supposed to have their source in the psychology of the person. But if we surrender to feelings of this kind we are thoroughly deceived. Reductionist explanations are not unprofitable, but they make only borderland gains. Mainland sociology is committed to explaining social facts by social facts.

The second observation is that we are only needled to seek for explanation by some sense of puzzlement. We are not motivated to have everything explained, because there are already many things in our experience that fall into place. Once something is well enough explained, the relationships it has with other things become part of its definition and description. As a consequence, our priorities in research are largely decided by our practical perplexities, so there is much unevenness in research. But this fact has another possible implication for sociology. It is often charged that the findings of some sociological study were already known to common sense. This may indeed mean that sociology is not yet equipped to delve deeply. But there is also the possibility that we may already possess a good deal of sociological understanding. Although sociology is a young science, there is nothing new for man in the experience of living in society. Might it possibly be that when the full explanatory account of human society is written down a sizeable portion of it will be written—"with acknowledgments to common sense"? Is it just possible that our sense of making meager progress in sociology is partly due to a large original advantage?

chapter 3

Explanatory Theory, Analytical Theory, and the Ideal Type

To have a *theory* about anything is to have an explanation for it. To achieve that is the goal of science, and a discipline has no *theory* until it has a coherent explanation for the things it studies. Yet other more modest theoretical components come into one's work in the course of the search. Although these are by no means "theories" they are part of one's theoretical armamentarium. It is important that we give recognition to them and know where they fit. We are somewhat at a loss to designate them, though, once we decide not to call them *theories*. For they express theoretical rather than empirical concerns. Essentially, their work is to sort out our world by developing concepts. Perhaps the way out of the difficulty is to call this whole area of operations *analytical* theory. This would distinguish it from *explanatory theory*, and it is of the utmost importance that we remember the definite dividing line between these. Needless confusion and recrimination have invaded sociological discussion through forgetting it. A common mistake is to think that assembling analytical concepts is tantamount to having a *theory* in the explanatory meaning of the word. When anyone who has come under this illusion learns his mistake it is even possible that he will blame the subject instead of himself. For instance, the work of Talcott Parsons has been overwhelmingly in the domain of analytical theory. It does not have the power to explain social phenomena and does not purport to do so. Its great virtue is to make us vividly aware of what is meant by *the social* and to name some of the components of it. Although this is not the end of a science, it is its quite indispensable beginning. It seems utterly obtuse, then, for anyone to blame Parsons

24

for not having brought us to El Dorado in a day, when he has done so valiantly to get us launched. You cannot cook the goose until it is dressed.

Actually, the "theoretical" accomplishments of sociology so far have been preponderantly at this level. There is a considerable wealth yet to be counted in concept formation in the discipline. A major project for "theoretical" work in sociology still is to take stock of its concepts, refine their definitions, and link them up together. Without apology, I envisage the present work as a contribution to this important task. It involves no contradiction, surely, to acknowledge that explanatory theory is the ultimate goal of our science and to insist that we come to it by stages, each of which must be vigorous in itself. It is also necessary that we find the route whereby we pass from conceptual to explanatory theory. This could prove quite a delicate maneuver. Before naming our sociological concepts, then, we will give some attention to the way they operate in our exploration of the actual world and in generating the terms for an explanatory theory of it. This brings us to a fresh assessment of the importance of heuristics and of the ideal type in particular.

A heuristic is the first match struck in the darkness. *Heuristics* refers to the processes of finding out, to search procedure, or, as it has also been expressed, to progressive thinking. It is not the window-dressing of the published report, but our fumbling and blundering—and self-correction. Possibly the heart of it is our sensitizing to relevant differentiation: in a hitherto grey world what is it that begins to stand out as significantly distinct? We attempt to give it a face.

Max Weber recommended the *ideal type* as a heuristic for adoption in sociology.[1] This is a notion that has never been entirely clear, and Weber's interpreters have scarcely succeeded in making it clearer. Every field of study probably generates its own kind of heuristic in response to the phenomena in it. What Weber proposed for sociology reflects his profoundly voluntaristic view of social action. In his view, social structures are what men make them: they are the products of purposive choices and actions. The ideal type of a social activity, then, is the drawing out of the implications for action of a particular commitment, were the commitment to be followed consistently toward its logical conclusion. Weber appreciated that when a group decides that something is worth accomplishing, a whole *set* of activities has to be started in order to accomplish it. These diverse activities have to elbow their way in, competing with other things for time and support, and so on. They therefore may or may not come to their full unfolding. Whether they do will depend on a variety of things: the strength of dedication of the people concerned, the strength of their competing aims, their knowledge,

[1] M. Weber, *The Methodology of the Social Sciences*, trans. and ed. E. A. Shils and H. A. Finch (New York: The Free Press of Glencoe, Inc., 1949).

their resources, any outside opposition to what they are trying to do, and so on. But it is not difficult to imagine what the full unfolding of their position would be, if its growth were unimpeded. And this precisely is the ideal type of it. It is the utopia of the undertaking. In the course of a few pages, Weber describes the ideal type as a "utopia" a number of times. This is an appropriate way of summing up what he was aiming to convey and it possibly contains the whole clue to his meaning. It should have received more attention.

The ideal type is a utopia in this sense: it is what the sociologist believes the people under study would be striving for, were they unfettered by the compromises of life. It is quite likely they will never have conceptualized a utopia for themselves, but that would not prevent his imputing one to them. On the other hand, it is just as likely they will have defined their own utopia. For often a group will have its constitution or charter, policy, program, or official statement of aims. These are just the kinds of tendencies Weber recognized to inhere in social action, and the sociologist makes use of them in fashioning his ideal type. The ideal type may sometimes resemble these tendencies very closely, although it remains the sociologist's construction in the end. It should be made clear, of course, that the ideal type is not the sociologist's ideal *for* anyone, it is not something he wants to enjoin on anyone. It is closer to his ideal *of* them. That is, it is his most sympathetic picture of them according to his understanding of what they want for themselves. It is in this sense that their actions, attitudes, etc., are *idealized*.

In everyday life we continually use such ideal types to guide our thinking and action. Why, for instance, do we so often express astonishment at what people do? It is because we feel it is inconsistent with the commitment we understand them to have made. "Fancy you missing the biggest match of the year, I thought you were a real sporting man!" "Fancy you joining the Army, I thought you were a Quaker!" "Fancy you not drinking tea, I thought you were an Australian!" What is being outraged in all three instances is our ideal type. We sometimes allude disparagingly to this as using "stereotypes." Yet they are indispensable to us. The stereotype of life and ideal type of sociology are very close to one another. Rightly used they are of advantage to us: it is only the abuse of them we have to avoid. We misuse them if we forget that individual cases will diverge from type, or if we refuse to modify the type when there is mounting evidence that it is a false image. Our approach to people and situations is insightful insofar as our store of accurate stereotypes is rich. It is by the use of the same insightful procedure that Weber himself has given us ideal types of bureaucracy, feudalism, patrimony, asceticism, mysticism, charismatic leadership, and other things besides.

Weber's pure type of bureaucracy will serve to illustrate his procedure.[2] It itemizes a set of characteristics. Weber believed that in committing themselves to the bureaucratic form of centralized administration, people would strive to implement certain practices. There would be a definite hierarchy of officials. Their jurisdictional areas would be strictly defined by rule. There would be a large staff of clerks to deal with records. Systematic training would be provided for the holders of executive offices. The official would regard his role as a calling that might oblige him to surrender all his working capacity to it, even though his obligatory time in the bureau may be delimited. The whole system would be run by stable rules that could be learned by those involved in it. Complexes of behavior that exhibit all these features measure up to the ideal type, those that deviate in any way are impure.

But if the ideal type is a fiction not necessarily found in life, how do we decide what to include and exclude in compiling it? It is clear that we take our cue from real life in the first instance, yet probably not so much from what is being done as from what is being aimed for. Weber says the ideal type is an *"accentuation* of one or more points of view."[3] I hardly think we should accept this if it meant a falsification through exaggeration. We could scarcely entertain a caricature. Nor could I concur if it meant the observer placing the accent according to his selective interest in the subject: there could be no end to the diversity and arbitrariness such an approach would license. Rather, we should try to discern what the *people observed* are accenting, where *they* are "putting their emphasis," as we say. It is this that gives distinctive direction and character to their striving and entitles us to name it. Thus we come to adopt terms like *Methodism,* or *reaction,* or *socialism,* or *university.* Starting with that observation, we observe further what array of practices is gathered up in the train of different cases where the same end is pursued. This observation may indeed be impressionistic and intuitive, yet it is still empirical observation. We compile our ideal type from this composite image. We keep the elements that are common to all cases except that we reject any that are inconsistent with the aim, and we may add others of our own imagining that would be consistent and swell the complement. Yet this ideal type is nothing in itself. Sometimes it seems to be assumed that this is the whole end of sociological investigation—to get some ideal types—and that law-finding or theory-building have no place. But this is a grave misunderstanding, for developing an ideal type is simply part of a heuristic procedure, a

2 H. H. Gerth and C. W. Mills, eds., *From Max Weber: Essays in Sociology* (London: Routledge & Kegan Paul, Ltd., 1952), pp. 196–244.

3 Weber, *The Methodology of the Social Sciences,* p. 90. Copyright 1949 by The Free Press.

stage on life's way. Weber defined its function picturesquely: "It serves as a harbor until one has learned to navigate safely in the vast sea of empirical facts." [4]

Built up in the way I have described, the ideal type is a rational construct, and Weber stressed this. We keep in it or put into it actions that are rationally required by the end in view. We think it sensible to do so because experience convinces us that rationality is one of the conditions of successful social action. Although the ideal type is a fiction, then, it is not idealized in any purely arbitrary way. It is commended to us as a measuring rod for actual cases. But there would be no virtue in measuring a case's deviance from a purely arbitrary norm. The ideal type is a relevant standard for measuring social phenomena because it measures a case's degree of self-realization. It is measured against what it might be and would need to be if it is to be of maximum effect.

If I am representing it correctly, then, the ideal type is nothing more than a collection of traits that we expect could occur together. We so expect partly because we have found empirically that some of them do, but partly also because we have a general theoretical expectation that other rationally-linked traits will be joined with them, the goal in view being what it is. So we expect, shall we say, that *A, B, C, D, E, F, G,* and *H* will occur together. Yet it is scarcely correct to call this our hypothesis: it is really never correct to equate ideal type and hypothesis. For when I say we measure actual cases against this, what we do is to see how many and which of these traits occur together in fact. We use the ideal type to ask this further question: How far have the exigencies of reality allowed this principle to unfold—this principle of feudalism, communism, democracy, or whatever it may be. We will doubtless find that in fact it has been hemmed in, compromised, cut off in mid-career, got so entangled with other principles as to be obscured, perhaps riddled with inconsistencies. Yet if such imperfections occur not randomly but systematically our ideal type will have led to a hypothesis. If the same blemishes begin to recur quite regularly on the pure type we will begin to suspect that is the shape of reality. We will come to assume that these are the things which probably do occur together, irrational though some of it may be. Of the traits above, perhaps only *A, B, D,* and *H* are found together and, although we had hardly expected it, *X* and *Y* besides. Once we are convinced of this pattern we adopt it for our hypothesis and can throw the ideal type away. It was meant to be expendable. We may leave the harbor now, for we have learned to navigate in the sea of empirical facts. We have not yet proven anything, but we are launched with a hypothesis.

4 *Ibid.,* p. 104.

There seems to be a pathetic lack of fulfilment about the ideal types of sociological literature. They have been too readily accepted as the end of the search instead of the means of searching. We still look back to Weber's ideal types of bureaucracy, charisma, religious rejections of the world, and so on, as though we had graphic pictures of phenomena. We consider them somewhat idealized for artistic effect, but graphic pictures nevertheless. Yet Weber never intended ideal types to be regarded that way. He meant us rather to ask, concerning them: Are the real cases altogether like this, or are they quite systematically otherwise? Like the grain of wheat that falls into the ground and may die, an ideal type only bears fruit if it yields a hypothetical type. Very likely it will yield several. We then think it worthwhile to test for the existence of these hypothetical types. If, after testing, we establish them (or something like them) as factual, we may have arrived at an empirical generalization or explanation schema. For now we may demonstrate a constant relation between a single event or set of events and their causes. This will be possible if one or more traits make their appearance in advance of the others. The passage from analytical theory to explanatory theory will have been made. It is imperative that we take note that in making this passage the definition of our terms has almost certainly undergone a change; at least we will have to be sure whether that has happened or not. If we go on to crown the conjunction of empirical elements with a nonempirical explanatory variable, this variable will take its definition from its empirical matrix. *Reaction* as a general exploratory concept is an ideal type; *reaction* as a nonempirical explanatory variable intervening between empirical observations is not an ideal type and has probably changed its meaning. In any case it is *reaction* as it is defined by reference to things observed. The whole entanglement at the theory-research junction may be a reflection of neglecting to realize this. Yet Robert Winch drew attention to the importance of recognizing the distinction between heuristic and empirical typologies in 1947.[5]

The fulcrum of the argument of this book is that the meaning of a given term used in explanatory theory is not the same as the meaning of the same term used in analytical theory. Hence the terms of analytical theory cannot enter into explanatory statements, as such; they must be transformed. Even if the collections of traits for the ideal type and empirical type are ultimately identical, the latter represents a configuration found in the real world. This cannot be guaranteed of the former (and is not in fact asked of it).

An instance of radical revision of the ideal type to make it applicable to empirical data is Johnson's revision of the Troeltsch-Weber church-sect typology.[6] In Johnson's opinion, the original typology is "applicable only to a specific historical context" and "encompasses a variety of elements which tend to vary independently." [7] Through using the typology he becomes convinced that reality diverges from it systematically. For an empirical classification of "most groups in the Jewish, Christian and Islamic tradition" and of the "major religious groups of the United States," [8] Johnson consequently resorts to something that salvages only one basic distinction in the previous typology. "A church," he proposes, "is a religious group that accepts the social environment in which it exists." [9] Actually, in spite of the explicit disavowal, Johnson appears still to assume that there are *some* constant organizational features distinguishing the sect from the church. If this were not the case, his one-factor typology would have little point. What he seems to want to imply, at the explanatory level, is that acceptance or rejection of the social environment gives rise to distinct forms of religious expression. Now there is nothing in this denouement of Johnson's thinking to bring Weber's types under a cloud. *They were ideal.* It is an index of their fruitfulness that they helped Johnson to form a conclusion about actual cases.

Another instance of revision of the ideal type that might be given is the author's modification of Zimmerman's familistic-atomistic typology for the family.[10] Zimmerman imputed six main characteristics to the familistic family:

> Its features were (i) a large number of children; (ii) close solidarity with kinsfolk and neighbourhood, with a resulting acknowledgment of the right of kin and community to prescribe what constitutes proper family conduct; (iii) the transmission between generations of a traditional concept of family roles and of one's place in society; (iv) strong ties of dependence between family members because of the family's multiform functions (including the maintenance of its own property, the family estate); (v) members' acceptance of family control over their behaviour and of authority within it; and (vi) a high valuation on family life and unity. In the atomistic family of the modern city, in which members are considered to be mainly bent upon

[6] B. Johnson, "On Church and Sect," *American Sociological Review*, **28** (1963), 539–49.

[7] *Ibid.*, 539.

[8] *Ibid.*, 539.

[9] *Ibid.*, 542.

[10] H. Fallding, "Inside the Australian Family," in *Marriage and the Family in Australia*, ed. A. P. Elkin (Sydney: Angus & Robertson, 1957). See C. C. Zimmerman, *Family and Civilization* (New York: Harper & Row, Publishers, Inc., 1947).

egoistic satisfactions, these *structural* aspects are said to be no longer strong.[11]

An empirical investigation of urban families suggested that the first four of these factors may be tied together without the last two being necessarily tied with them. The last two may occur both in the presence and absence of the first four. The implication, at the explanatory level, is that urban living had caused a weakening in the first four factors, whereas the last two were independent of it. What this finding does, in effect, is supplant a six-factor ideal type by a four-factor empirical one. But the ideal type guided the inquiry.

Finally, we may, by way of contrast, take note of a radical denouement where the empirical testing of an ideal type leads not to a modified empirical type but to abandonment of the scientific stance altogether. Studying Tepoztlán seventeen years after Redfield's investigation, Lewis sought to discover whether changes in that period conformed to the folk-urban typology of social change that Redfield had introduced.[12] According to this type, any increasing urban influence on a village community is accompanied by increasing disorganization, secularization, and individualization. Lewis did not consider that this constant combination of factors was confirmed. As a consequence, he abandons the attempt to characterize village community change in terms of *any* constant combination of factors, falling back on a method that takes fuller recognition of the unique features of different historical periods. To anyone committed to a science of society this is disappointing, for it amounts to something like an admission of failure. Historical data are as good for sociology as any other sort of data, but the use made of them is almost opposite the historian's. We know that historical periods exhibit different phenomena but we would still like to know whether they have features in common—and if they do, what those features are. Our disappointment is increased by Lewis' suggestion that he need not have been so radical in dismissing the method of searching for types. Perhaps he could have settled for an empirical type through modification of the ideal type in the manner I have been advocating. For in one place he states, "On the whole, many of our findings for Tepoztlán might be interpreted as confirming Redfield's more general finding for Yucatan, particularly with regard to the trend toward secularization and individualization, perhaps less so with regard to disorganization." [13]

11 Fallding, *op. cit.*, p. 55. Reprinted by permission of the publisher.

12 R. Redfield, *Tepoztlán—A Mexican Village* (Chicago: The University of Chicago Press, 1930); R. Redfield, *The Folk Culture of Yucatan* (Chicago: The University of Chicago Press, 1941). See O. Lewis, "Tepoztlán Restudied: A Critique of the Folk-Urban Conceptualization of Social Change," *Rural Sociology*, 18 (1953), 121–37.

13 *Ibid.*, 130. Reprinted by permission of The Rural Sociological Society.

We should not assume that ideal types are always present or necessary in sociological inquiry. We may simply compare one case with
another to find out what they have in common. Howard Becker did
this, for instance, in his "constructed typology" of a marginal trading
people.[14] In his study diverse peoples were shown to exhibit three traits
in common: expedient rationality, emotional aloofness from out-groups,
and economic internationalism. These were exhibited by the Jews,
Armenians, Parsees, some Chinese in the Dutch East Indies, some Greeks
in Egypt, and certain lowland border Scots. This cluster of three traits
is a hypothetical type arrived at directly by comparison, without the
mediation of any ideal type at all. Becker is virtually suggesting, then,
that we test for a constant association between these factors because
they have already been found to occur together in some actual cases.
He stresses that the constructed type occurs nowhere in actuality—and
yet this triad does. What he probably means is that the triad does not
occur bare, without other trappings attached, and that these trappings
may be different for different cases. That is, it is *abstracted* from reality
as all the generalizing concepts of science are; but it is not idealized.
Yet it is a pity that Becker failed to distinguish his constructed type
from the ideal type more deliberately than he has. They have often
been taken for the same. In a footnote, Becker even says his constructed
type is an ideal type, similar to but not identical with Weber's. Yet his
reason for avoiding the term *ideal type* is not because he wishes to differentiate his notion from Weber's, but because of the misunderstandings that can attach to the word *ideal*. As if to further confuse us, in
the same essay Becker reproduces his typology of religious organizations:
ecclesia, sect, denomination and cult—all ideal types in the Weberian
sense. He goes on to suggest that you can propose and test hypotheses
about these types: for example, that the cult is transformed into the
sect. But we cannot do that until we have given these terms an empirical
definition. The only immediate thing we *can* do is ask how far actual
cases correspond to or diverge from the type.

Becker's discussion of the generation of types is illustrative of the
prevailing lack of clarity on the subject. Two recent commentaries on
the practice show the same thing. They appear to be in direct contradiction with one another, the latter written actually claiming that is
the case. McKinney uses the term *"constructed type"* and acknowledges
what I have said to be the case—that this type is the potential basis of
an explanatory schema.[15] If he intends to exclude all reference to the

14 H. Becker, "Constructive Typology in the Social Sciences," in *Through Values
to Social Interpretation* (Durham, N.C.: Duke University Press, 1950), pp. 93–127.

15 J. C. McKinney, "Methodology, Procedures and Techniques in Sociology," in
Modern Sociological Theory in Continuity and Change, ed. H. Becker and A. Boskoff
(New York: Holt, Rinehart & Winston, Inc., 1957), pp. 186–235.

ideal type, what he says is unexceptionable, but it is doubtful that he means to do this. Martindale maintains that if McKinney is referring to the ideal type he has misunderstood it.[16]

All in all, the ideal type has been exposed to more than its share of misunderstanding. Perhaps this is because it occupies a place in a line of succession. It is a heuristic that abdicates at the appointed time in favor of a hypothetical type, which in turn abdicates in favor of an actual type—and this last may constitute an explanation. If we lose sight of this denouement, and fail to know where we stand at any point, we can misjudge the ideal type because we have first misrepresented it. Yet, rightly understood and handled, the progression from the ideal type to the actually demonstrated type is one of the most rewarding avenues that can be followed in sociological research. It is a research design that is born of insight and has theory as its goal. To negotiate the passage, however, requires a great deal of painstaking and wisely planned empirical work, and it may take generations—even centuries— to do so. Have not sociologists in general expected to come into their inheritance far too quickly, even with magical speed? As a science, sociology is still more a proposal than an achievement. Notions like Parsons' pattern variables and Merton's modes of adaptation,[17] for instance, are ideal types that imply a program of long-continuing work. Whole generations may have to work in the field before they wring hypotheses from them. And explanatory theory about these matters lies beyond that again.

The ideal type, as a case of the heuristic, resembles what is now called a *model*. That term has been variously employed, of course, much to the confusion of us all. Brodbeck has reviewed its different uses by sociologists, but makes no useful recommendation about a desirable restriction of use.[18] Nagel's usage is one of the most precise, and yet it seems narrower than that which has useful currency now.[19] He makes *model* refer simply to the mental imagery with which we clothe our theoretical entities in order to have some pictorial grasp of them: we say the molecule is like a ball, the social system like an organism. In regarding new and strange phenomena we believe we see a patterning

16 D. Martindale, "Sociological Theory and the Ideal Type," in *Symposium on Sociological Theory*, ed. L. Gross (Evanston: Row, Peterson, 1959), pp. 57–91.

17 T. Parsons, *The Social System* (London: Tavistock, 1952), pp. 68–112; R. K. Merton, "Social Structure and Anomie," in *Social Theory and Social Structure* (New York: The Free Press of Glencoe, Inc., 1961), pp. 131–60.

18 M. Brodbeck, "Models, Meanings, and Theories," in *Symposium on Sociological Theory*, pp. 373–403.

19 E. Nagel, *The Structure of Science, Problems in the Logic of Scientific Explanation* (New York: Harcourt, Brace & World, Inc., 1961), pp. 106–17.

similar to old, familiar ones. These are essentially analogies, yet they do more than help us visualize; they help our thinking to unfold by taking it in new directions. For them to be useful it is not necessary to believe that the molecule *is* a ball or that society *is* an organism. Nor need our suppositions from them involve the logical fallacies of argument by analogy. Furthermore, our theoretical entities are ultimately defined abstractly by the relations in which they stand to one another—so once we have used a model to imagine them the model is expendable. The model is, as it were, a scaffold for concept-building, but no integral part of conceptualization. Nagel points out that electromagnetic theory, which led to the positing of an "ether," satisfactorily explained many experimental laws and predicted many phenomena. But even the nineteenth-century physicists who used the theory never imagined that it implied the real existence of "ether."

But *model* now seems to be used in a broader sense than this. It is taken to mean a system of concepts that is useful in mapping the variables in a field under investigation. It may be a corner of the field or the whole field of the subject: a model may be of bureaucracy, for instance, or of society in general. In the latter case, the system of concepts in its entirety makes a heuristic for the deductive theory in its entirety that we hope to achieve in the end. For in scientific work we do not start out with an empty mind, nor even with isolated hypotheses. We start with a guess about the whole structure of our universe of discourse. The coherence that goes into this system of concepts, a coherence whereby each concept is defined by the relationship in which it stands to the others, is analogous to explanation but is not explanation in fact. For it is not an account of reality as it has been experienced. Something like this is what has now come to be called a model, although it has also been common to call it a conceptual scheme. Recently in sociology it has fallen from favor. In the next chapter, I try to restore the model or conceptual scheme to dignity.

chapter 4

"Grand Theory" Vindicated
and "Theory of the
Middle Range" Reconsidered

In the 1950s the air became thick with exclamations against "grand theory." Yet we should reappraise this commotion. What precisely was being attacked and what was being proposed in its place? The attack was not quite the same thing in all quarters. In some cases it even seemed to involve a confusion.

Merton, you might say, started it all.[1] He was the first to point out that all was not running well in the sociological household. In 1949, he wrote:

> Throughout [*Social Theory and Social Structure*] I attempt to focus attention on what might be called *theories of the middle range:* theories intermediate to the minor working hypotheses evolved in abundance during the day-by-day routines of research, and the all-inclusive speculations comprising a master conceptual scheme from which it is hoped to derive a very large number of empirically observed uniformities of social behavior.[2]

Merton continued:

> From all this it would seem reasonable to suppose that sociology will advance in the degree that its major concern is with developing theories of the middle range and will be frustrated if attention centers on theory in the large. I believe that our major task *today* is to develop special theories applicable

[1] R. K. Merton, *Social Theory and Social Structure* (New York: The Free Press of Glencoe, Inc., 1961), pp. 5, 6, 9.

[2] *Social Theory and Social Structure*, pp. 5–6. © 1961 by The Free Press.

35

to limited ranges of data—theories, for example, of class dynamics, of conflicting group pressures, of the flow of power and the exercise of interpersonal influence—rather than to seek at once the "integrated" conceptual structure adequate to derive all these other theories. The sociological theorist *exclusively* committed to the exploration of high abstractions runs the risk that, as with modern *décor*, the furniture of his mind will be sparse, bare, and uncomfortable. To say that both the general and the special theories are needed is to be correct and banal: the problem is one of allocating our scant resources. I am suggesting that the road to effective conceptual schemes in sociology will be the more effectively built through work on special theories, and that it will remain a largely unfulfilled plan, if one seeks to build it directly at this time. So it is that in his inaugural address at the University of London, T. H. Marshall has lately put in a plea for "sociological stepping stones in the middle distance."

That this emphasis may be needed can be seen from a review of books on sociological theory. Note how few, how scattered and, it must be said, how unimpressive the instances of specific sociological hypotheses which are *derived* from a master conceptual scheme. The basic theory (or speculation) runs so far ahead of confirmed special theories as to remain an unrealized program rather than a *consolidation* of apparently discrete theories.[3]

It may be significant that Merton was proposing a time strategy: priorities for *that day*. Even so, we may question whether he diagnosed the trouble correctly. That there was trouble is probably beyond question, for it can be granted that theory and research were out of touch with each other. Yet Merton seems to have taken the conceptual scheme for the deductive theory. He speaks as though he wanted us to hold back, whereas he really wanted us to move forward into the realm of explanation. He misrepresents this desire as a wish not to embark on a general deductive theory too soon. Possibly it is largely from this statement of Merton's that the notion of "grand theory" as premature deductive theory has gotten abroad. Yet we need never fear we will produce a deductive theory before time, need we? For we would never invent one except in the attempt to explain laws at hand. Any deductive theory we then devise could be wrong, but it could scarcely be premature. It would hardly be able to achieve a wide range until it had passed through the middle ranges first. It is by definition unnecessary, then, to make any plea for theories of the middle range.

Many who came after have made a refrain out of Merton's cry.

3 *Ibid.,* p. 9.

In 1954, Zetterberg took up the cudgels for "miniature theories," equating these with "theories of the middle range." [4] Yet there is little point in his labored defense of them when his conclusion is that inclusive theories are more easily formulated in fields that have miniature theories first. He sees the attainment of inclusive theory as the goal and more or less guaranteed. It appears his main concern is not inclusive theory, but that we should leave preoccupation with definitions and frames of reference. By undertaking verificational studies rather than merely descriptive ones we can move on to explanation, he says. Now this is entirely in line with the thesis of this book. Yet we cannot afford to lose sight of the fact that studies of co-variance demand a continuing concern with the definition of the variables. Concern with verification and concern with frames of reference are scarcely in competition with one another: they are mutually supporting.

In his Preface to *Class and Class Conflict in Industrial Society*, Dahrendorf claims his book will exemplify "theory of the middle range." [5] By this he means two things: its subject matter will be restricted, viz., to industrial society; and its theoretical generalizations will arise from concrete observations. The main point, surely, is not the range of the theory but that it will be theory that attempts to explain known facts. Even so, it is interesting how much of this book has to be given to defining the concept *class*. Dahrendorf finds this entirely necessary before he can go on to present explanations of class phenomena.

The lion raging beyond the wall of grand theory was of course C. Wright Mills.[6] He did not, however, advocate "theory of the middle range" as a way out. Presumably that was because he did not see "grand theory" as theory of great range. In attacking "grand theory" he was inveighing against a sterile arrestment at frames of reference. He was tormented by everyone's seeming inability to make capital out of these:

> The basic cause of grand theory is the initial choice of a level of thinking so general that its practitioners cannot logically get down to observation. . . .
>
> One resulting characteristic is a seemingly arbitrary and certainly endless elaboration of distinctions, which neither enlarge our understanding nor make our experience more sensible. This in turn is revealed as a partially organized abdication of the effort to describe and explain human conduct and society plainly.

[4] H. L. Zetterberg, *On Theory and Verification in Sociology* (New York: Tressler Press, 1963), pp. 10–16.

[5] R. Dahrendorf, *Class and Class Conflict in Industrial Society* (Stanford, Calif.: Stanford University Press, 1963).

[6] C. W. Mills, *The Sociological Imagination* (New York: Oxford University Press, 1959).

When we consider what a word stands for, we are dealing with its *semantic* aspects; when we consider it in relation to other words, we are dealing with its *syntactic* features. I introduce these shorthand terms because they provide an economical and precise way to make this point: Grand theory is drunk on syntax, blind to semantics. Its practitioners do not truly understand that when we define a word we are merely inviting others to use it as we would like it to be used; that the purpose of definition is to focus argument upon fact, and that the proper result of good definition is to transform argument over terms into disagreements about fact, and thus open arguments to further inquiry.[7]

Mills is justified, of course, in clamoring for explanation. Yet I would suggest that the paralysis Mills notes is attributable, not to the choice of an overgeneral level of thinking, but to a failure to see that the terms of analytical theory are ideal types and can only be the terms of explanatory theory if they are transformed.

We may take as a final expression of dissatisfaction with the state of sociological theory an outburst from George C. Homans.[8] In a footnote he says he is thinking particularly of the work of his colleague and friend Talcott Parsons:

> Much modern sociological theory seems to me to possess every virtue except that of explaining anything. Part of the trouble is that much of it consists of systems of categories, or pigeonholes, into which the theorist fits different aspects of social behavior. No science can proceed without its system of categories, or conceptual scheme, but this in itself is not enough to give it explanatory power. A conceptual scheme is not a theory. The science also needs a set of general propositions about the relations between the categories, for without such propositions explanation is impossible. No explanation without propositions! But much modern sociological theory seems quite satisfied with itself when it has set up its conceptual scheme. The theorist shoves different aspects of behavior into his pigeonholes, cries, "Ah-ha!" and stops. He has written the dictionary of a language that has no sentences. He would have done better to start with the sentences.[9]

This seems to be altogether correct, except for the final sentence. Homans gives due recognition to the need for a conceptual scheme, but warns that it does not make an explanatory theory. Like Mills, he does

---

[7] *Ibid.*, pp. 33–4.

[8] G. C. Homans, *Social Behavior, Its Elementary Forms* (New York: Harcourt, Brace & World, Inc., 1961).

[9] *Ibid.*, pp. 10–11. Reprinted by permission of the publisher.

not join in any refrain for "theories of the middle range." Yet he can hardly be serious when he suggests we would do better to start with explanatory propositions and leave our terms undefined. There is no evidence here, either, of an understanding that the terms of explanatory propositions differ from those of the conceptual scheme in that they take their definitions from the real world.

There is much to indicate that serious students of society are intent on explanatory theory as the end of their search. But if this leads to a rejection of conceptual or analytical theory it leads them into error of the gravest kind. If they misconstrue such theory for explanatory theory of wide range, they may advocate theories of the middle range instead. But this involves a misunderstanding and in any case makes a redundant plea. The issue is not the range of the theory but the kind. We stand in need of explanatory theory, but cannot have it until we have quantitative observations to explain. For explanatory theory accounts for the world of experience. Preliminary to a comprehensive explanatory theory is a mountain of research. And yet, to give everything its due, the world of our experience has no semblance of order and, indeed, poses no questions unless we know the ways in which it may be differentiated. It is here that analytical concepts, defined as ideal types, play their exploratory role.

It may be instructive to compare studies by two men who are especially dedicated to explanatory theory for sociology. I refer to George C. Homans' *The Human Group* and Neil Smelser's *Theory of Collective Behavior*.[10] Although they are motivated by the same kind of concern, these books deliver contributions to knowledge at different levels. Comparing them illustrates how necessary it is for the discipline to produce on both levels. It may also remind us that any contribution will have the limitations of its strengths. Let us consider Smelser's book first.

Smelser identifies a set of elements which may conspire in releasing or containing an episode of collective behavior: situational conduciveness, structural strain, generalized belief, precipitating factors, mobilization for action, and social control. These work cumulatively by what Smelser calls a *value-added process:* each must be active for the next to become operative. Smelser also analyzes situations in terms of values, norms, the mobilization of motivation in roles and organization, and facilities. He says that, whereas these components of social action give a "language for describing and classifying action," the value-added process gives "a means for organizing determinants into

10 G. C. Homans, *The Human Group* (New York: Harcourt, Brace & World, Inc., 1951); N. J. Smelser, *Theory of Collective Behavior* (New York: The Free Press of Glencoe, Inc., 1962).

explanatory models." [11] It is not entirely clear how far he means this latter claim to go. I would allow that it may *ultimately* lead us to an explanation of many phenomena in the field of collective behavior, but I do not think it constitutes this yet. It is, precisely, an ideal type of collective behavior (and most probably this is what Smelser intends his claim to mean). It has within it the germ of an explanation were its terms ever to be transformed into empirical ones. One could not say that it constitutes even an hypothesis yet.

This is because Smelser's method is simply to illustrate the separate elements of a process from the literature on collective behavior. He says he has used systematic comparative illustration, but in fact the illustrations are very random and, more to the point, they are fragmentary. Any real case is invoked to illustrate only one or several phases of the total process. Smelser does not here take a set of cases and examine each one for *all* elements in the process he defines. This is the next, necessary step before an explanatory theory of collective behavior could come out of this work. The book, in fact, prescribes a plan of further exploration entailing enough work for a regiment. It bids us take many cases of each variety of collective behavior and ask of every one whether and how the identified elements conspire to produce their effect. Are the real phenomena consistently linked in the way that Smelser says, or are they quite systematically otherwise in any way? To say this in no way detracts from the importance of Smelser's contribution. I have suggested that this imaginative phase is the highpoint of scientific endeavor. Also, the work still to be done cannot necessarily be expected from one man, and it is also quite possible that such work may have to wait on new data.

To digress for a moment, it may seem surprising that collective behavior can be rendered as an ideal type in view of the facts that I have stressed the rationality of the ideal type and that collective behavior is usually characterized as irrational. Yet we may doubt whether collective behavior is as irrational—in the sense of lacking practical rationality—as is supposed. As Smelser depicts it, collective behavior is essentially an adaptive reaction to strain, an attempt to repair damage— the reaction, however, of the impatient. Because it short-circuits the journey from generalized belief to specific situation, it may effect a very clumsy adjustment, and therefore contrasts with those more rational processes where these intervening steps are thought out. Rather than call it the action of the impatient, it might be even better described as the action of the pushed. For it is their *situation* that compromises the actors. They are victims of an objective limitation more than a

11 *Ibid.,* p. 383.

subjective one. Whatever their action lacks in rationality is not due to their lack of patience so much as to their lack of time. The ideal type of collective behavior is therefore no less a "rational construct" than other ideal types. It is constructed with an awareness of the need for practical rationality in human action and is shaped to show wherein this need may be honored in the circumstances and wherein it must be denied.

Homans, too, has his components of action in *The Human Group:* activity, sentiment, norm, and interaction. At the most general level, these make a model or ideal type of the group itself, as do Smelser's components of action. But there is nothing in Homans' study to parallel Smelser's value-added process: there is no set of elements defined by their relationship to one another to give us an ideal type of group operation. Homans begins by analyzing one case only and then compares several. Without the use of an ideal type at all, hypotheses are developed that connect the components. Persons who interact frequently will develop sentiments of liking, persons who feel sentiments of liking will engage in extra activities, the higher a person's rank in a group the greater will be his conformity to its norms—and more of this kind. Homans is aware that it is the connections between hypotheses that bring coherence and comprehensiveness to any explanatory theory achieved. He is also aware of what a slight contribution his own study makes to a full explanation of societies and their component groups. Not one but two deficiencies have to be made good: the hypotheses must be tested in many more groups; and there have to be many additional hypotheses "for an adequate analysis of even the simplest human group." [12] Exactly like Smelser, Homans has work enough for a regiment. He would hardly claim to have done more himself than illustrate a method for getting it done. We may admit Homans' contribution to the realm of explanatory theory, a distinction we had to deny Smelser's. But we should note at the same time the different limitation imposed by his method of work. Because he gives us no ideal type, we cannot locate the given hypotheses in any shadow matrix of possible supporting ones. His determination to entertain nothing but the empirical renders him tight-fisted toward us, for he offers no help in finding the many additional hypotheses he calls for. We are on our own.

More power to explanation. That it is king nobody will deny. But there is a certain naïveté in imagining we will reach a general explanatory theory through special ones—unless we take care. Our special theories will have to be given in the same terms as one another if they are ever to be put together. Separate explanations of the family, religion, govern-

12 Homans, *op. cit.,* p. 443. Reprinted by permission of the publisher.

ment, education, and crowds, for instance, will scarcely add up unless
they are given in common terms. It is the role of conceptual theory
("grand theory" if you like) to help find those terms. It is also imperative, of course, as was said at the very beginning, that these terms be
distinctively sociological. It is time for us to consider wherein the
distinctiveness of social facts lies.

part 2

*Empirical Measurement
by Evaluation of Function*

chapter 5

Social Facts

Durkheim justified a distinct science of sociology on the ground that social facts exist in their own right.[1] He had a time defending himself against ridicule because he made his claim as well as his definition of social realities very explicit. Max Weber was partner to the same revolution in employing the notion of social action, but did it quietly and consequently provoked less resistance.[2] Strictly speaking, sociology both as discipline and profession has as its sole *raison d'être* the elucidation of social facts. Yet some within the camp seem to have as little understanding of social facts as many without. Much work that has been done under the name of sociology lies closer to psychology, for instance. Homans has suggested that the movement Durkheim fathered is already spent, so little was there to it.[3] I would claim, on the contrary, that we have scarcely begun to understand what Durkheim wanted from us. Moreover, we do not need to be forever held up asking if we will follow Durkheim. We could go further than Durkheim in the direction he showed us. To study social facts is difficult indeed, as Durkheim in any case warned, and too often those who set out with that intention regress into more familiar modes of thought. They collect data, but think about it geographically, or historically, or philosophi-

[1] E. Durkheim, *The Rules of Sociological Method,* trans. S. Solovay and J. Mueller, ed. G. E. G. Catlin (New York: The Free Press of Glencoe, Inc., 1950).
[2] M. Weber, *The Theory of Social and Economic Organization,* trans. A. M. Henderson and T. Parsons, ed. T. Parsons (New York: The Free Press of Glencoe, Inc., 1947), p. 88.
[3] G. C. Homans, "Bringing Men Back In," *American Sociological Review,* **29** (1964), 809–18.

cally, or economically, or demographically, or psychologically, or even ideologically—but to think sociologically seems to be too much to ask. Then again, applying the findings of these other disciplines to life is sometimes thought to constitute sociology, as if sociology were nothing but the art of scientific living—and by every science, apparently, except a science of society itself.

The difficulty of studying social realities is not that it may require masses of data that only a team can muster. For some problems this may well be necessary, but you can view a social fact in a single person. Part of the reason for regressing from sociology into psychology, in particular, may be that we have our own subjectivity to witness to the reality of the things psychology studies. On the other hand, the sociological facts of which we are the vehicles are often things of which we are barely conscious. But the main reason why the study of social facts is difficult is that the sociological point of view is difficult to sustain. Sociological vision comes by training. Yet without this vision we are blind to powerful forces. It should be understood why anyone calls attention to the separate existence of social facts: it is not that they are more important than the facts reported by other disciplines, but that other disciplines do not touch them. We do not deny, say, psychology to establish sociology. It is just that when the psychology of a situation has been given the whole tale is not told. Our aim is to complete knowledge.

There are three intellectual orientations that can sometimes put scales on the eyes and make it virtually impossible for a person to achieve the sociologist's vision of society. Each of these approaches enables us to gain a certain kind of understanding, but can inhibit sociological understanding if made oversufficient. Purely for the sake of having names by which to refer to them, I will tag them the *numeralist*, the *nominalist*, and the *synthesist* approaches. They will each be considered in relation to what I understand to be the authentic approach of the sociologist.

I use the term *numeralism* for the view which holds that if society has a real existence at all, it is a numerical one: the total number of individuals in an area or under a government, say, or that proportion of any such population which has a certain characteristic, such as a specified age, height, income, history of disease, country of birth, and so on. Those who take this enumerative view of society are inclined to equate the study of society with the collection of census-type information and the making of surveys. Anything on a big scale like this is considered sociology, anything on a small scale, like the intimacy of a couple, is, apparently, taken to be psychology. This outlook embodies a very inadequate conception of society. But there can be a degree of sociological sense implicit in it on occasion. For often the counts are made within units which are sociologically real (in the sense shortly to be explained)—within the nation, say, in which all those counted bear the role of citizen, or within the working class, the farming sector, the armed forces, married women, and so on. This enumerative notion of the social is one that Durkheim thought important to refute. He said that the universal repetition of some trait in the members of a society or sector of it was not what made it social. It was only social if it had appeared everywhere because it had been made standard and imposed by sanction.

Numerical analysis of populations is most characteristically under-taken by demography. A number of writers have recently concerned themselves with the status of this study as a systematic science, and with the question of whether it has systematic connections with the studies on which it impinges, and with sociology especially.[4] The general conclusion is that demography focuses on man's quantity and sociology on his social organization, so that they should be neither equated nor confused.[5] It has also been pointed out that demography is not necessarily any closer to sociology than to such other natural or social sciences as genetics, economics, psychology, and geography; and the fact that "demography has become largely a sub-field of sociology for instructional and academic housekeeping purposes in the United States is more a matter of historical accident than of special affinity."[6] At the same time, the continued association between demography and sociology is cordially anticipated in sociological literature, as this will facilitate the search for connections between variables from the two orders.[7] But there have been warnings that no direct leap can ever be made from demographic data to sociological conclusions, for the former are not ordered within the theoretical categories of sociology.[8] It is, of course, imperative to add that professional demographers may exceed *bare* demography at the outset. They may address themselves to problems of social organization and disorganization, as these are affected by population factors.

By *nominalism* I mean the view that only psychological processes have any reality in "what we call" society, and that society is "the name

4 See, for instance, P. M. Hauser and O. D. Duncan, eds., *The Study of Population: An Inventory and Appraisal* (Chicago: The University of Chicago Press, 1959).

5 P. M. Hauser, "Demography in Relation to Sociology," *American Journal of Sociology*, **65** (1959), 169–73; and G. A. Hillery, Jr., "Toward a Conceptualisation of Demography," *Social Forces*, **37** (1958), 45–51.

6 Hauser, *op. cit.*, p. 170. Reprinted by permission of the University of Chicago Press.

7 *Ibid.;* and Hillery, *op. cit.*

8 R. G. Francis, "The Relation of Data to Theory," *Rural Sociology*, **22** (1957), 258–66.

we give" to the interaction of two or more individuals. This interaction has no properties of its own apart from the properties of the
individuals who mutually influence one another. Society is thus to be
thought of as a field of interpersonal forces, and even this is only a visual
aid or a way of putting it: there are really only the individuals, each
of which can be a cause of changes in the others. This is the type of
outlook exemplified in the attack F. H. Allport made some time ago
on what he called "the group fallacy." [9] Largely outmoded now, it is
nevertheless an outlook for which there is a lag of unconscious bias.
Holders of this restricted view, however, are seldom aware of how pre-
cariously they ride. If you start dissolving the rarer layers of reality,
where do you stop? If anyone is entitled to say that society is not real
because he has not been arrested by the importance of its *emergent*
properties, one can say with equal justification that the mind and
personality are not real, that behavior is not real, nor the human body,
nor matter, nor motion, nor energy. This kind of thing comes down to
 limiting the world to whatever our eyes have become most accustomed
to looking at. It is, of course, the well-known fallacy of reductionism:
the unnecessary denial of a higher-order reality in order to safeguard
recognition for a lower order incorporated in it. The charge that we are
reifying if we think social facts real but not if we think psychological
facts real is tiresome. We reify no less when we impute a nature to a
person or even to a natural object. It is in the economy of thought and
action always to assume that anything in experience has its peculiar
reality.

Even if one avoids both the numeralist and nominalist fallacies,
one can still have difficulty distinguishing between the proper realms
of sociology and psychology. Social psychologists seem a good deal less
clear than demographers about how their study articulates with sociology.
This question has probably never been treated with all possible thorough-
ness and precision. Some writers even seem to have a vested interest in
keeping the issue beclouded. Nevertheless, several things are clear about
the necessary procedure for solving the problem. First, as Sprott has
pointed out, we should not define a subject by who does it.[10] The professional psychologist and sociologist may each ask questions in the
other's field. But if a psychologist applies himself to a sociological question this does not make it psychology. It would be no solution at all
to throw together everything produced by professional sociologists, for

[9] F. H. Allport, "The Group Fallacy in Relation to Social Science," *American
Journal of Sociology,* **29** (1923), 688–706; and "An Event-System Theory of Collective
Action," *Journal of Social Psychology,* **12** (1940), 417–45.

[10] W. J. H. Sprott, *Human Groups* (Harmondsworth: Penguin Books, 1958), p. 19.

instance, and say, "What you see emerging here must be what sociology is." We have to define things on a basis of principle. By the same token, we cannot be dependent on having a worker himself tell us just where he is ranging. Because he is a psychologist or because he may want to aggrandize his discipline, or for other reasons, a psychologist may call sociology psychology. Finally, then, the field we are in is determined by the question we ask. It is what we are trying to explain that matters, not simply what data we have in front of us. I might have before me measurements of a group's cohesion and an individual's anxiety. What field am I in? No particular field at all. If I ask, "Why is this group's cohesion low?" I am in sociology. If I ask, "Why is this person's anxiety high?" I am in psychology. With the data in hand, then, I can move into each field in turn. And I may even explain each set of data by the other. I may answer that the group's cohesion is low because one individual is anxious and this has made him obstructive. This is sociology. It is also possible I may answer the second question by saying that the individual is anxious because he lacks the support of a cohesive group. This is psychology. If there are questions whose answering uses variables from two fields, the questions still belong to either one field or the other: specifically, to the field of the dependent variable. There is therefore a psychological sociology (our first answer belongs to this) as well as a social psychology. If this seems a pedantic point, it is nevertheless a clarifying one.

It can fairly be claimed that what is published under the caption "social psychology" is strictly speaking either psychology or should be returned to sociology. The reader will be forewarned, then, if he remembers that *sociology* as I shall define it may well claim part of the work of social psychologists and some of the material reported in the social psychology texts. Much that is apt to be treated there under socialization, interpersonal relations, group dynamics, group norms, public opinion, and crowd behavior I consider sociology. Although it sounds cynical to say it, parts of these texts read like padding introduced to bolster the impression that social psychology is a separate major science. Yet I believe there is a proper social psychology and that it speaks on all these matters. For instance, Newcomb, Turner, and Converse raise a question in social psychology when they ask whether the manifestation of an *ability* to lead, which could remain dormant, is determined by social conditions.[11] (Their answer is that holding positions of power or visibility may have that effect.) And they make one observation in social psychology when they report that a condition of successful brain-

[11] T. M. Newcomb, R. H. Turner, and P. E. Converse, *Social Psychology, The Study of Human Interaction* (New York: Holt, Rinehart & Winston, Inc., 1965), p. 483.

washing is an authority's assumption of something like total control over the person;[12] and another when they report that a shared acceptance of a norm has the effect of internalization in the person, so that the norm becomes self-enforcing there.[13] Shibutani reports a fact of social psychology when he says that stable sentiments, like affection or resentment, result from the interpersonal roles people play.[14] But he is wrong to suggest that the study of interpersonal roles belongs to social psychology rather than sociology simply because interpersonal roles can be distinguished from conventional roles. We are confronting super-individual phenomena as much in the one case as in the other.

Furthermore, as I draw the line, any social psychology that is rightly so called is a branch of psychology, not of sociology. It has a connection with sociology and I would, of course, want to see it taught in sociology departments. But it is probably less misleading to represent it as an adjunct or auxiliary to the study of sociology than as a branch of it. On the practical level, the situation is chronically confused, precisely because courses and books in social psychology contain sociology. Roger Brown, for instance, is very reluctant to give a definition of *social psychology* at all, but goes so far as to concede that it "is concerned with the mental processes (or behavior) of persons insofar as these are determined by past or present interaction with other persons."[15] Now this definition, like other formal definitions given in books, is one with which I am in full accord. Yet Brown's text covers much more than this— and a great deal of it enters into sociology.

In a similar way, Newcomb, Turner, and Converse say their aim is to formulate their problems in terms of "psychological processes which take their particular form from the interactional context in which they occur."[16] There could not be a more acceptable statement of the task of a social psychology: mental processes—the dependent variables—are to be considered as they are determined by interactions—the independent ones. Such a study would be misnamed, however, if it were subtitled *The Study of Human Interaction,* as it is. For by any ordinary understanding, when we speak of the study of anything we mean the attempt to explain it, not making reference to it to explain other things. A page later, however, the authors tell of their varied departmental memberships, apparently taking pleasure in the fact that none of them could conceive of formulating any of their central problems in terms of either

12 *Ibid.,* p. 112.

13 *Ibid.,* pp. 242–50.

14 T. Shibutani, *Society and Personality, An Interactionist Approach to Social Psychology* (Englewood Cliffs, N.J.: Prentice-Hall, Inc., 1961), pp. 323–66.

15 R. Brown, *Social Psychology* (New York: The Free Press of Glencoe, Inc.; London: Collier-Macmillan, 1965), p. xx.

16 Newcomb, Turner, and Converse, *op. cit.,* p. v.

sociology or psychology alone: "It is no accident that we have so often resorted to schemas in which collective variables are now viewed as independent and individual ones as dependent, and a moment later the other way around." [17] This is fine. But it simply means that, in spite of their purer aim, they will be treating us to both social psychology and psychological sociology in turns. This can lend an aesthetically pleasing stereoscopic depth to their presentation. But we should not be deluded into thinking that we have, on the level of systematic science, anything except explanations in two separate disciplines. One particularly misleading tendency of psychologists is to represent any study that is behavioral or any study of interaction on a small scale as social psychology. But social facts can be studied behaviorally too, and all relationships down to that of a pair are social phenomena.

In trying to differentiate sociology from psychology, people also get hung up on "the individual," which they consider the exclusive preserve of psychology. But "the individual" is an abstraction belonging to both disciplines, according to how he is regarded. True, sociology is concerned with superindividual realities, but they are carried on individuals. Durkheim himself probably generated some of the misunderstanding in this regard. In fact, Durkheim's notion of social psychology seems to have been two things rather than one, neither of which coincides with my own. In one place, he says that the task of social psychology is to establish the laws of collective thinking.[18] This is a reference to what would today most likely be called the sociology of knowledge. But Durkheim also asserted that the "individual manifestations" of social phenomena are not sociological phenomena in the strict sense of the word. "They belong," he wrote, "to two realms at once; one could call them sociopsychological." [19] Now this statement masks a confusion, I believe. I would say that social phenomena are partly manifested in individual persons; and to the extent that they are, individual manifestations of social phenomena *are* sociological phenomena. But the impress on the mental life of the person of his participation in the larger life is a psychological phenomenon. The difference lies in the boundaries within which we confine the behavior for definition (though not necessarily for explanation). If we locate an individual's behavior in the person, we view it psychologically; if we locate it in the interactive process to which it contributes, we view it sociologically. In short, the line that divides sociology from psychology splits "the individual." Insofar as Homans refers to this when he demands that we "bring men back in," I have no objection to his approach. There have to be indi-

---

17 Newcomb, Turner, and Converse, *op. cit.*, p. vi.
18 Durkheim, *op. cit.*, p. li.
19 Durkheim, *op. cit.*, p. 8.

viduals if there is to be society. But I certainly would not accept this if it meant bringing psychology into sociology. There *is* a psychology of every action performed in society, but it can be left unspoken so far as the science of society is concerned.

As a subject of sociology, the individual is a contributor to collective states, and there are doubtless a great variety of methods by which individuals can be viewed to study them in this capacity. In *The Rules of Sociological Method*, Durkheim recommended one method for assessing collective states: to measure the rates at which members of a collectivity exhibit a particular behavior. He believed that this would show how far and in what different ways the group coerces its members or leaves them unconstrained. Yet, judging by Durkheim's demonstration of the method in his study of suicide, rates require considerable interpretation before they can speak for states.[20] We would handicap ourselves needlessly, however, and in a way Durkheim would not approve, if we restricted ourselves to this as the only method for obtaining social facts. Mott begins his textbook by demonstrating how rates have been used to indicate social states, but quickly passes on to point out that many sociologists "study and analyze the characteristics of social organizations without any reference to rates of behavior." [21]

At this point, I shall characterize society as the sociologist sees it; we will then be in a better position to consider the *synthesist* approach. Society, in the view of the sociologist, is a state of organization of joint activity. *The Structure of Social Action*, the title of a book of Talcott Parsons,[22] translates the whole matter into a formula. *Social action* was Max Weber's term,[23] but Parsons claims to have detected a convergence on this understanding of social behavior in a group of writers. Weber saw society distinctly enough simply by viewing the individual; for individuals live in social situations—there are others around them. For any person to act at all is to take these others into account. His actions are meaningful to him in terms of the relations they are seen to effect. Social action is quite simply action with this orientation and sociology is the science of it. I do not at all conclude from this that Weber doubted that social facts exist over and above psychological facts: it simply means that he considered the individual *as actor* a social fact. A reciprocity of interaction is implied by social action,

[20] E. Durkheim, *Suicide, A Study in Sociology*, trans. J. A. Spaulding and G. Simpson, ed. G. Simpson (London: Routledge & Kegan Paul, Ltd., 1952).

[21] P. E. Mott, *The Organization of Society*, © 1965. By permission of Prentice-Hall, Inc., Englewood Cliffs, N.J.

[22] T. Parsons, *The Structure of Social Action, A Study in Social Theory with Special Reference to a Group of Recent European Writers* (New York: The Free Press of Glencoe, Inc., 1964).

[23] Weber, *op. cit.*

so that *social interaction* makes an alternative short title for the subject matter of sociology. But the social action of the individual is the simpler element. A variety of things, indeed, are implied by the fact of social action, and it has been one of Parsons' major contributions to track many of them down, especially in *The Social System*.[24] One of the most evident is that social action tends to become structured; that is to say, it assumes a prescribed and so predictable form—and hence the appearance of the term *structure* in Parsons' title. Repetition of action is often taken to define social structure, but this is scarcely essential to it, although very common. What is important is that the action transpires over time and is controlled in its course. If for no other reason, structuring occurs because others demand to know what they are to expect. But the actor simultaneously demands to know what he is to expect of others; so, strictly speaking, no one's social action is structured except insofar as it engages the social action of another. Thus there is an interlocking of joint activity in differentiated roles.

People engage in joint activity to procure the things they think will satisfy their common needs. The activity becomes increasingly organized (elaborates a structure) as roles and their accompanying statuses are distributed among those who take part. The distribution takes shape under the influence of shared beliefs that it ought to be thus and not otherwise; and these normative beliefs, recorded in some symbolic way, constitute a culture. Social organization and culture are the floor and ceiling of the sociological house and together make an order of things that has properties of its own. This order comes into being, develops, and breaks down through superindividual forces that are not the mere sum of the individual psychologies underlying them. To explain and even describe this world we therefore need special concepts and methods. If we were to apply demographic or psychological methods, for instance, the whole fabric would slip through our grasp: sociological knowledge would not be attained. It would therefore be absurd to urge sociologists to use these methods because they are more rigorous and objective. Sociologists must develop rigorous methods appropriate to their data or else be deflected from their course.

The requisite methods are those that will uncover the structure and functions of social systems, for all units of joint activity have definite boundaries supplied by the action itself, which make it possible to treat the action as a system. There is, moreover, a tendency for social activities to aggregate in units so as to economize effort. To speak of the structure of social systems is to refer (at the very least) to the pattern of the roles within them; to speak of functions of social systems is to

24 T. Parsons, *The Social System* (London: Tavistock Publications, 1952).

refer to the ends accomplished, wittingly or unwittingly, through joint activity. In the kind of society to which we are ourselves accustomed, there are four main organizational levels at which systems of action make their appearance; or so Parsons has recently suggested [25]—and I follow him here. There is first what he calls the *technical* or *primary* level, where people produce something in face-to-face association. Then there is the *managerial* level, where their activities are coordinated through supervision in large-scale organizations. Next is the *institutional* level, where some kind of pervasive norms and leadership coordinate and standardize, at least to a degree, the action taken in the diverse organizations concerned with some basic need—say education, religion, health, material provision, and so on. And finally there is the *societal* level, where the whole community of people endorses political action for the coordination of their many institutional practices. The core of the subject matter of sociology is the examination of systems on levels such as these.

It can confidently be claimed that this is the orthodox conception of the subject of sociology today, and the one that gathers up its most incisive traditions. It is not one position among vigorous competitors. It has built on foundations laid not only by Durkheim and Weber but also by Pareto, Radcliffe-Brown, and Malinowski.[26] If men like Parsons and Merton have been most vocal in expounding its principles, it is only because they have expressed the whole trend of thought common to their contemporaries.[27] One does not have to be a "Parsonian" to side with Parsons: one only has to be a sociologist. Davis has argued, for instance, that it is a myth that functional analysis is a special method

[25] T. Parsons, "General Theory in Sociology," in *Sociology Today: Problems and Prospects,* ed. R. K. Merton, L. Broom, and L. S. Cottrell (New York: Basic Books, Inc., 1959), pp. 3–37.

[26] V. Pareto, *The Mind and Society: A Treatise on General Sociology,* trans. A. Bongiorno and A. Livingston with the advice and active cooperation of J. H. Rogers, ed. A. Livingston (New York: Dover Publications, Inc., 1963). A. R. Radcliffe-Brown, *Structure and Function in Primitive Society: Essays and Addresses* (London: Cohen & West, 1952) and *A Natural Science of Society* (New York: The Free Press of Glencoe, Inc., 1957). B. Malinowski, *The Sexual Life of Savages in North-Western Melanesia,* 3rd ed., with Special Foreword (London: Routledge & Kegan Paul, Ltd., 1932); "Culture," in *Encyclopaedia of the Social Sciences* (New York: The Macmillan Company, 1937); *The Dynamics of Culture Change, An Inquiry into Race Relations in Africa* (New Haven: Yale University Press, 1945); *Argonauts of the Western Pacific, An Account of Native Enterprise and Adventure in the Archipelagoes of Melanesian New Guinea* (New York: E. P. Dutton & Co., Inc., 1953); and *A Scientific Theory of Culture, and Other Essays* (New York: Oxford University Press, 1960).

[27] R. K. Merton, *Social Theory and Social Structure* (New York: The Free Press of Glencoe, Inc., 1957) and "Social Problems and Sociological Theory," in R. K. Merton and R. A. Nisbet, eds., *Contemporary Social Problems, An Introduction to the Sociology of Deviant Behavior and Social Disorganization* (New York: Harcourt, Brace & World, Inc., 1961), pp. 697–737.

in sociology and anthropology—it is, rather, *synonymous* with sociological
analysis.[28] Recent criticisms of Parsonian functionalism show that social
systems are more open than Parsons explicitly acknowledged. But his
generic conception of the social system persists, and it would show a
complete lack of perspective if anyone supposed that these criticisms
have dislodged Parsons' work from its central place.

The only important competing scheme for an overall conceptualization of society which I am aware of is the ecological one. But this was
an incredibly naïve approach, for it ignored the elementary sociological
fact that culture renders man to a high degree immune to direct environmental influences. And it is perhaps significant that the pioneer
ecologists studied *man in the city,* apparently considering the city as the
environment. But the city is part of man's culture, and is thus not an
environment in any strict use of the ecological idea. But for the fact
that they looked at populations rather than single individuals, their
approach could almost be termed that of social psychology. It is my
belief, however, that Burgess virtually signed the resignation of this
fashion in thought when, in his "Introduction" to Shaw and McKay's
Juvenile Delinquency and Urban Areas (1942), he interpreted delinquency and the other factors which occurred with it as symptoms of
social disorganization.[29] Of course, it was almost certainly not realized
at the time that, in turning the ecologists' thoughts in this direction,
Burgess was weaning them from some of their basic assumptions. Also,
I mean no derogation of their superb contribution to sociology when
I say that their theoretical formulations at this point were weak. For
the Chicago ecologists were better than their principles, and the flimsy
ecological mantle with which they clothed their solid sociological observations was not essential to them.

There are two main difficulties about sociological work that keeps
on flogging the ecological idea. One is that the idea is given so many
meanings. The other is that the idea is never made into an instrument
that can clamp hold of a fact. The things described elude the grasp
of the term, and one cannot help feeling they would be equally well
described if it were not hovering over them at all. But one can say even
more than this. They would be better described if the spatial aspects
of social organization were treated under the cultural norms that give
organization its form. If there is a time and place for everything, it
is because men think certain times and places appropriate. They *allocate*
times, places, and spaces to their various activities in accordance with

28 K. Davis, "The Myth of Functional Analysis as a Special Method in Sociology
and Anthropology," *American Sociological Review,* 24 (1959), 757–72.

29 C. R. Shaw and H. D. McKay, *Juvenile Delinquency and Urban Areas* (Chicago:
The University of Chicago Press, 1942), pp. ix–xiii.

the priorities the activities have in the total society. It is a mistake to think of social organization sitting in an environment like a cup in a saucer; rather, the environment is swallowed up in the organization. Firey's polemic against the earlier ecology was designed to show all this, and he recommended a new "cultural ecology." [30] This seems almost a contradiction of terms, and it might have been better to drop the term ecology at that point. Presumably Firey maintained it simply to designate the traditional set of problems, even though he was repudiating the traditional point of view on them. Schnore's thinking shows a trend very similar to Firey's.[31] He stresses how important it is for urban ecology to focus on the structure and function of urban activities. But this is really the same kind of abdication of the ecological stance that Burgess and Firey exhibited. In *The Urban Scene,* for instance, what power does the environment get? It is plastic in men's hands to be shaped according to their knowledge of it.

Of all uses of the ecological concept, Hawley's is the most profound.[32] He would not use Firey's definition, for instance. Firey stated: "Social ecology is concerned with explaining the territorial arrangements that social activities assume. Its task is to discover and to explain the regularities which appear in man's adaptations to space." [33] Hawley cited a definition of the same variety from McKenzie, only to reject it because of its superficial accent on space.[34] If human ecology were to mean anything analogous to biological ecology, Hawley believed, it must refer to the fact that a species adapts to an environment and survives only as a collectivity. A collectivity engaged in a common struggle to maintain and expand life makes a community. Human ecology, then, is essentially the study of the cooperation of the human community, this cooperation not being exclusive of internal adjustments through conflict. But there is a certain bathos in Hawley's *Human Ecology.* The book does not fulfil its promise to apply the ecological concept as the author defined it. Hawley's definition of *community* demands that it be equated with "ecological organization" on its broadest base. In the modern world, it is clearly the nation that constitutes the effective community in Hawley's sense, although there are international extensions of it as well. It is the nation that is organized to maintain and expand life. But at the point in the book where he wants

---

[30] W. Firey, *Land Use in Central Boston* (Cambridge, Massachusetts: Harvard University Press, 1947).

[31] L. F. Schnore, *The Urban Scene: Human Ecology and Demography* (New York and London: The Free Press of Glencoe, Inc., 1965).

[32] Amos H. Hawley, *Human Ecology—A Theory of Community Structure* (New York: The Ronald Press Company, 1950).

[33] Firey, *op. cit.*, p. 3.

[34] Hawley, *op. cit.*, p. 69.

to apply his concept to data, he takes his definition of *community* from everyday speech, and from there on it means a local settlement. Using "community" now with that meaning, he tries in vain to defend his deflection from his task:

> For our purposes community has essentially the same meaning as ecological organization, the one difference being that the former is applied to a relatively small unit of territory whereas the latter may extend over an area of indefinite scope. Formally defined, community refers to the structure of relationships through which a localized population provides its daily requirements. In some instances the bounds of ecological organization and of community are coterminous, in others ecological organization extends well beyond the limits of a single community embracing two, three or any number of communities. The chief advantage in dealing with the community is in that it offers a relatively small and convenient unit for investigation.[35]

The subterfuge and disappointment of Hawley's treatise consists in this: whereas he set out to transform the everyday definition of community into "ecological organization" as he defined it, he finally allowed the latter to contract to the former. This is a great pity, for the concept of community as cooperation in struggle seems to be the one that has most sociological potential. Finally, although Hawley felt some workers had too high a view of culture in differentiating man in the animal kingdom, there is little doubt he himself had too low a view. To Hawley culture was simply an instrument of environmental adaptation. But culture builds finer things than that into its edifice. I will shortly argue that it is a unity man fashions to maximize satisfaction through the achievement of meaning and dignity. What Hawley's approach permits us to focus on is really the material economy, and it is the organization of this that remains the subject matter of ecology when the ecological mantle is stripped away.

It is certainly the material economy that is explored in *Metropolis and Region*.[36] This book by Duncan and his collaborators is very self-consciously ecological. Yet what it amounts to finally is a study of the spatial differentiation of the industry of a nation: if it has any community for its subject, it is the American people. Although the authors cannot document the process as they would like, it is a chief implication of their study that no city or region in which industry operates stands alone,

[35] *Ibid.*, p. 180. Copyright 1950 The Ronald Press Company, New York.
[36] O. D. Duncan, W. R. Scott, S. Lieberson, B. Duncan, and H. H. Winsborough, *Metropolis and Region* (Baltimore: The Johns Hopkins Press, 1960).

so far as industry goes. There is a nationwide flow, a system of interconnections. Thus the idea of differentiation by local environment is over-
ridden by an idea that a total effort exists, a system to which local industry
is tributary.

Finally, also, we have to recognize that the economy remains the political economy still. Resources can only be allocated in the ways authority
sanctions, so an exploration of economic organization may well involve
consideration of the political organization as well. Studies of the provision
of material needs may therefore be studies of political organization.
Rossi and Dentler focus on this in their study of urban renewal in
Chicago.[37] And they phrase their problem wholly as one of action and
influence. It is a relief to say that there is not much ecology here and that
the study has greater substance as a result.

Let no one misunderstand this criticism of "ecological" sociology.
I do not mean to imply that the things the ecologists study are unimpor-
tant or that their work is unprofitable. The organization of the material
economy is as important as anything in sociology. The allocation of space
is important; from the practical point of view, it could be critical for our
urban civilization. I am only saying that the studies are inappropriately
conceived and in any case have revealed a shift to the kind of conceptualization I claim to be orthodox. Some ecologists complain that their work
is denied a place in the mainstream of sociology. If so, it is not because
of what they choose to study, but simply because they write sociology in
a quaint dialect that calls for constant translation. Why not drop the
foreign term *ecology* from sociology altogether, and treat the same matters
under different headings? "Economic organization," "political organization," and "community" would seem to cover most of them. Mumford,
for one, is able to cover this area without the ecological paraphernalia.[38]
Contrast the vividness of his approach with the flatness and elusiveness
of the ecologists'. True, one wonders at Mumford's confidence in judging
all he describes, and I do not mean to commend him in everything; but
he sees cities as cultural creations made by man as a home and is consequently able to draw them in depth.

There is even another school of sociologists who feel uneasy about
the position I have called orthodox and who stand apart from it, although
they offer no alternative scheme for an overall conceptualization of so-

37 P. H. Rossi and R. A. Dentler, *The Politics of Urban Renewal, The Chicago
Findings* (New York: The Free Press of Glencoe, Inc., 1961).

38 L. Mumford, *Technics and Civilization* (New York: Harcourt, Brace & World,
Inc., 1934); *The Culture of Cities* (New York: Harcourt, Brace & World, Inc., 1938);
City Development, Studies in Disintegration and Renewal (London: Secker & Warburg,
1947); *The City in History, Its Origins, Its Transformations, and Its Prospects* (New
York: Harcourt, Brace & World, Inc., 1961); and "Regional Planning and the Small
Town," *Journal of the American Institute of Architects,* **14** (1950), 3–10, 82–91.

ciety. It is exemplified by men like Rose and Mills [39] and by the proposition that society is "process." They feel that the notion of a system is too static to allow a reasonable analysis of social change, and they are even inclined to suspect that it may be a cloak for political conservatism. One sympathizes with their stress on change, for continuous change is a social imperative; but so also is some degree of stability. I further submit that some of the crucial problems of social analysis concern the tactics people devise to reconcile these requirements. It seems sociologically perverse to think that recognition of one implies a denial of the other.

One of the most vigorous defenders of the reality of social facts in early American sociology was Small, and he thought they were best apprehended as process—to him a process of developing, adjusting, and satisfying people's wants, the *raison d'être* of interaction.[40] Structures are generated in interaction as a means to this end and might function either well or badly in achieving it. Setting up wants (or needs) as a kind of judge over structure and function in this way is a thing I wholly endorse, as I shall show later in the book. There is, indeed, a fatal futility in studying systems if we fail to take into account the products they yield and the appositeness of these products to people's needs. It was partly to secure recognition of this that Small insisted on a primacy for process. But he had another concern besides. With Ratzenhofer, he recognized that conflict of interests may sometimes rupture the accommodation of interests on which structures rest.[41] Perhaps it is mainly to force a greater recognition for either or both of these things—need-satisfaction and conflict—that criticisms of the "systems approach" have arisen. Yet a recognition of them is not excluded by the systems approach. For, as Hawley states, wants have to be achieved collectively. A man in search of satisfaction always has some fellows: no one ever got much, if anything, by being at war with all. Even in conflict there is concern, at the very least, with an in-group order, probably with a larger order than that. For if men do not choose to annihilate their enemies entirely (and they seldom do), then they choose to subjugate them by *rule*. The inescapable conclusion is that there is virtually no satisfaction of wants except through systems, and no discernible social process apart from the emergence and decay of systems that arise to service these wants. We are faced with a

39 A. M. Rose, ed., *The Institutions of Advanced Societies* (Minneapolis: University of Minnesota Press, 1958), pp. 3–42. C. W. Mills, *The Sociological Imagination* (New York: Oxford University Press, 1959).

40 A. W. Small, *General Sociology, An Exposition of the Main Development in Sociological Theory from Spencer to Ratzenhofer* (Chicago: The Univerisity of Chicago Press, 1905).

41 G. Ratzenhofer, *Die sociologische Erkenntnis: positive Philosophie des socialen Lebens* (Leipzig: Brockhaus, 1898), and *Wesen und Zweck der Politik, als Theil der Sociologie und Grundlage der Staatswissenschaften* (Leipzig: Brockhaus, 1893).

kind of chicken-and-egg sequence. It is rather pointless, then, to say that
the social system and social process are alternative and opposed ways of
representing the subject matter of sociology. Each is so completely implied
in the other that either must be taken to mean both. For what is it that
changes in social process? Since we can scarcely conceive of man in an
original Eden where there is process without system, we have to say that
the social process is one system giving way to another. Reciprocally, when
we speak of systems we must also mean their emergence, decay, and transformation, and any conflict these entail.

Firth, in one of the most interesting attempts to conceptualize social
change, sees it as a short-term organizing response to a novel situation.[42]
A society, in his view, maintains a long-term stability in the background
of its life while setting up localized short-term (perhaps trial) arrangements at various growing points in the foreground. There is therefore
no need to suspect sociologists of unwarranted conservatism when they
are honest enough to recognize the social importance of stability. There
can be no doubt that every social arrangement, of any kind, is made with
some intention of conserving a stable patterning that will last until the
goal in view is achieved, or will satisfy recurring needs (men need food
every day, not once for all, and sleep every night), and that will relieve
anxiety by allowing men to anticipate that their future needs will be
supplied. Even the most politically radical do not want change for the
sake of seeing some capricious innovation for a day; they want change in
order to substitute new stable arrangements for existing ones. Think of
the ruthless suppression of counterrevolution and the Five Year Plans
and the like, implemented by what were originally revolutionary governments. What is a Five Year Plan but a stable arrangement for five years?

Finally, regarding varieties of sociology and their relation to the
orthodox, we must acknowledge the existence of a sociology conceived
as the study of social problems (as exemplified in the work of Booth,
Rowntree, Myrdal, and Mayo [43]), and of a sociology conceived as social
criticism (as exemplified in Veblen, Mumford, Riesman, and William H.
Whyte [44]). Yet, once again, neither of these approaches offers any different

[42] R. Firth, *Elements of Social Organization* (London: Watts & Co., 1961).

[43] C. Booth, *Life and Labour of the People in London* (London: Macmillan &
Company, Ltd., 1902–3). B. S. Rowntree, *Poverty: a Study of Town Life* (London: Mac-
millan & Company, Ltd., 1902) and B. S. Rowntree and G. R. Lavers, *English Life and
Leisure: a Social Study* (London: Longmans, Green and Co., Ltd., 1951). G. Myrdal
et al., *An American Dilemma: the Negro Problem and Modern Democracy* (New York:
Harper & Row Publishers, Inc., 1944). E. G. Mayo, *The Human Problems of an In-
dustrial Civilization* (Boston: Graduate School of Business Administration, Harvard
University, 1946) and *The Social Problems of an Industrial Civilization; with an
Appendix on the Political Problem* (London: Routledge & Kegan Paul, Ltd., 1957).

[44] T. Veblen, *The Theory of the Leisure Class: An Economic Study in the Evolution of Institutions* (New York: The Macmillan Company, 1899) and *The Instinct of*

scheme for the conceptualization of society. They may indeed make use of the one I have called orthodox, particularly if social disorganization becomes their concern. But a distinguishing characteristic of the former approach is that it tends not to sustain any systematic position, but collects data at a variety of levels according to the nature of interest in the problem—psychological or economic data, say, or information about material amenities, medical needs, and so on. And the distinguishing characteristic of the latter approach is an attachment to a particular view of human need which the person judges to be violated by the practices he attacks.

Having set aside its ailing rivals, let me return to a fuller characterization of the approach to society I am defending: sociology is concerned with practices that are undertaken with cognizance of their involvement in a system of action. These practices are said to be *institutionalized*—to use this notion now in the broader of the connotations given to it in sociology. Through institutionalization, raw *behavior* is transformed into *conduct. Conduct* is a more colloquial equivalent of Max Weber's *social action;* I am inclined to use it in place of that term, for, in this form, *behavior* is seen as a function of a social system rather than of an individual organism. Social systems are closed ovens which turn raw behavior to a digestible brown, the heat they apply for the purpose being the forces of socialization they sponsor. One side of what is involved in socialization is certainly a matter for psychology. But the sociologist is concerned with those socializing measures sponsored by social systems for their own preservation: rewards and penalties, and programs of initiation, training, and correction, have perhaps been the ones most commonly examined. But of profounder importance, surely, is the question of whether a system is so structured that individuals believe it clearly facilitates the satisfaction of some need—so that they can identify with it; or whether individuals feel that there are obstructions intervening, say because of factors like inefficiency, graft, exploitation, fossilization, ambiguity, and so on. Individuals can also withhold identification with a system, and so fail to be socialized by it, simply because they feel it does not maintain the liaison they look for with other systems in which their other needs are met. Now it is certainly true that only individuals can "conduct themselves," as we say. But they clearly would never adopt their various stances unless they acted opposite others in social systems. And

---

Workmanship, and the State of the Industrial Arts (New York: The Macmillan Company, 1914). Mumford, *op. cit.* D. Riesman, et al., *The Lonely Crowd: A Study of the Changing American Character* (New Haven: Yale University Press, 1955) and D. Riesman, *Individualism Reconsidered; and Other Essays* (New York: The Free Press of Glencoe, Inc., 1954). W. H. Whyte, *The Organization Man* (New York: Simon & Schuster, Inc., 1956).

the form of their conduct is decided by the expectations they come to share there with others, and not by themselves alone.

In *Science and Social Action,* Sprott undertakes to defend the distinctiveness of sociology as a subject of study.[45] To help him in this task, he analyzes the development of a shared expectation between two individuals. In a more concrete and entertaining way, he is echoing Parsons' examination of the basis of society in terms of the paradigmatic relation of a pair, alter and ego. Sprott writes:

> Imagine two friends who have been so related for some time. The actions of each when they are together are mutually adapted. After a while each can, as we say, "count upon" the other. In fact it is not merely that A can guess what B will do, as a psychiatrist can guess at the likely response of his patient, and it is not merely that B can guess what A will do, as, indeed, the patient may guess at the likely conduct of the psychiatrist. There is more to it than that. A knows that B knows what A is likely to do, and B knows what A expects B to expect. Something which one can call a mutually accepted system of expectations gets established. . . .
>
> The two parties may, of course, interact to their mutual satisfaction without either of them mentioning the matter either to the other or to himself. On the other hand, they may, when perhaps the expectations of one are falsified: "I never expected you to do such a thing" one might say; then what I have called the scheme of accepted values may become symbolized as "our friendship." Doubtless the symbol will be slightly different in one from what it is in the other; but there must be common constituents, otherwise neither will be intelligible to the other. Again, it might be that one of them wants to do something which will cause pain to the other, something indeed which conflicts with their mutual system. Then he may say to himself: "I really ought not," or even, "I really *cannot* do this or that. It would ruin our friendship." Suppose, for instance, it is their wont to go to the pictures every Saturday night. Suppose A has an enticing invitation for one Saturday night. Will there not be a conflict in A's mind? And, indeed, supposing both A and B receive an invitation for a Saturday night. Is it a gross exaggeration to suggest that they may say to one another: "Well, of course, it means giving up *our* Saturday night's pictures"? Something has been ever so slightly outraged. What, surely, has happened is that this day-to-day mutual scheme of inter-responses has become externalized and now stands out against them coercively. We are at once reminded of Durkheim's definition of a social fact: "Un fait social se reconnait au pouvoir de coercition externe qu'il exerce ou est susceptible d'exercer sur

45 W. J. H. Sprott, *Science and Social Action* (London: Watts & Co., Ltd., 1954).

les individus; et la présence de ce pouvoir se reconnait a son tour
soit à l'existence de quelque sanction determinée, soit à la ré-
sistanse que le fait oppose à toute entreprise individuelle qui tend
à lui faire violence. [A social fact is recognized by the power of
external coercion it exercises or is able to exercise on individuals;
and the presence of this power is in turn recognized, as the existence of some predetermined sanction or as a resistance the fact
poses to any single effort to violate it.]" [46]

Doubtless because of his legal training, Durkheim constructed his
vision of society around the coercion it exerts over the individual. This is
indeed a matter to wonder at, and a profound mystery still. While one
person may assert his interests over those of another, no one person assumes a moral entitlement over any other—but the group does, and a
single person may do so if the group makes him its agent. The group
defines the standards the individual must observe, as in lawmaking. These
standards are therefore experienced as coming from outside the person:
they have *exteriority*. Furthermore, the group applies *constraint*—punish-
ments and rewards—to enforce their observance. Conduct is thereby
standardized and so it is exhibited repetitively. The same members repeat
it on different occasions and different members do the same thing: it has
generality. (To avoid mistaking it for the notion of *generalization* used
in science and to keep Durkheim's essential meaning alive, I will call this
standardization.) Exteriority, constraint, and standardization operate to
produce "ways of acting" in a group, and these crystallize in time into
"ways of existing." [47] By *ways of existing* Durkheim appears to have meant
nothing other than the structural differentiation of social organization.
Thus he came to define sociology as "the science of institutions, of their
genesis and of their functioning." [48] Institutions, in turn, he defined as
"all the beliefs and all the modes of conduct instituted by the collectivity." [49] Yet if it appears from this that Durkheim only gave recognition
to firmly structured states in society, it must be pointed out that he also
saw social facts expressed in a less crystallized form, in what he called
social currents. These are the kinds of manifestation generally described
now as *collective behavior,* where a shared belief serves in the absence of
a division of labor to unify the group. Durkheim saw the whole range of
social forces operating very pervasively, wherever people associate. Yet
they were particularly vivid to him in child-rearing and education. Here
one could observe society very directly taking the individual in charge.

46 *Ibid.*, pp. 9–11. (Translation mine.)
47 Durkheim, *op. cit.*, p. 11.
48 *Ibid.*, p. lvi.
49 *Ibid.*

"The aim of education is, precisely, the socialization of the human being," [50] he said.

Coactivity in differentiated roles, shared expectation, exteriority of norms, constraint through sanctions, and standardization of practice—these five properties mark the *conduct* of the individual as a superindividual thing. It is probably correct to say that these are the ones Durkheim laid stress on. But at least ten more (italicized below) could be named. We might, for instance, dwell on the fact that the standards which prescribe acceptable conduct are there to safeguard the *continuance of association* as well as the *continuing supply* of whatever product is the fruit of the joint activity. This is true whether the standards are general or specific in their reference, superficial or profound—whether it is norms or values that are concerned, whether it is rules of etiquette, mores, or laws. Time is involved in the composition of groups, and a flow of gains is their fixed preoccupation. It is this permanence that invests the activity with an *identity* that can be symbolically represented as a name. Then again, the superindividuality of action develops a *resonance* that can gain an all-devouring intensity. By this I mean that the standards that safeguard joint activity are themselves to be counted among the products of joint activity. In fact, almost anything men make together is a standard, in that it has stamped into it an implication of how they ought to act toward it and toward one another through using it. Thus roads are for vehicles and not for tennis, bowling greens for sport and not for plowing up; the hammer implies that nails ought to be driven in by its use and not by the palm of the hand or the heel of the shoe; the automobile implies that this will be the means of transport in preference to the horse-and-buggy or go-cart. This self-binding of man by his technology illustrates a truth about all cultural products, whether they be tools or codes of law: the things men produce through superindividual activity tend very largely to be charters of commitment to yet more superindividual activity. Furthermore, if the new activities achieve independence of the old, there is *reproduction of a kind*.

The fact that in groups men are constrained by their own devices to make more devices further reminds us of the omnipresence of the artifact. Feibleman is one who has rightly stressed the importance of this.[51] He points out that every institution has *equipment*, and it is man's relation to this equipment as much as his relation to his fellows that gives the pattern to human action that constitutes society. It is as homo faber, not simply as homo sapiens, that we are concerned with man in sociology. This provides an important point of contrast with psychology. Because

50 *Ibid.*, p. 6.

51 J. K. Feibleman, *The Institutions of Society* (London: George Allen & Unwin, Ltd., 1956).

psychology locates the individual's behavior within his personal makeup for definition, it can leave the artifact out of account. But since sociology locates behavior within the system of action, it cannot. It is because of this that we can definitely refute the frequent assertion that "it all comes back to individuals in the end." The study of sociology does not come back that far: it comes to individuals *and* all the properties of their play. There would be no human life on earth at all if there were only individuals. Moreover, the fact that conduct is effected through the use of equipment (*facilities,* Smelser would call them) illustrates its *hierarchical ordering.* Equipment is usually employed as a means to an end. Individuals view each single act they perform as a means or an end, and the distinction observed in any instance is not forced on them by their intrinsic psychology but by the social task into which they are drawn. Earlier I said that the structure of systems consists in a patterning of roles, but this is a shorthand way of putting it. To discharge roles, individuals use equipment, which, we have seen, embodies standards—or norms as they might alternatively be called in this case. A role itself is a collection of norms specifying how anyone's efforts will dovetail with other efforts in the pursuit of ends. The ultimate standards, the ends of action—those satisfactions that are considered to be their own justification —these are values. Another way of putting it, then, would be to say that the elements of social structure are values and norms, while equipment and roles are instances of norms. Equipment, in the broadest use of the term, must be understood to include that instrument most precious to man, viz., knowledge. Roles are rated differentially according to where they come in the pyramid of roles effecting the end: they have status. Equipment gets a similar going-over: tools, for instance, are commonly lowlier and religious beliefs higher in the veneration earned.

The superindividual nature of conduct is also illustrated by the fact that cultural products are detachable from the actual presence of the groups who make them. Whether such products are as solid as furniture or as rarefied as religious beliefs, they all record an abstract idea in a material token—though the token be a book, say, or ceremonial vestment or sacrament, or even a spoken phrase vibrating in air. Although sociology cannot view man without his artifacts, it is certainly not interested in them in any gross sense, as material, but as his media for recording meanings. As such, they constitute a *symbolization of activity* and become a fluid currency that passes, possibly, to whole populations and generations of people who had no part in their making. Yet if these recipients accept the normative implications in them they subsequently become bound by them. Millions of workers who had no part in either the invention or manufacture of machines organize their entire working lives around them. Generations who may be largely ignorant of the founding fathers of their

nation will willingly conduct their lives within the constitution be-
queathed them. This *transmissibility of cultural symbols* is what makes
deliberate communication possible, and community through it. It is the
source of the social standardization of conduct within a society and it can
cause diffusion across cultural barriers. Because symbols detach standards
from any particular time and place, it becomes possible to reapply them
in every other time and place where they may be recognized to be appropriate. In two cities separated by the width of a continent the routines
of the post office may be virtually identical, and so may be those of the
Catholic church and the drugstore. Successive generations over centuries
may worship according to the same rites, marry according to the same
arrangements, show friendship by the same gesture, and enjoy conviviality
with the help of the same beverage. Thus the repeatability of conduct
through time and space can cause a vast honeycomb to spread out in both
of the two dimensions, and provide man with the at least relatively stable,
relatively predictable habitation without which he would apparently find
life intolerable and impossible.

It is into this structure of man's own devising, rather than into any
bare, unlined physical environment, that individuals are born. And it
implies no denial of underlying psychological realities to say that, from
this point of view, an individual is simply fluid material poured into the
honeycomb and that his life takes shape and meaning from the parts of
that structure—as a pillar of the church, cornerstone of the department,
bulwark of the movement; as a tower of strength to his associates, foun-
tain of wisdom, lever of influence—or even as everybody's doormat. Because we are concerned here with the moral and spiritual dimension of
life, any reductionism which would cut it down to the mental dimension
only would seem to be as morally, as it is intellectually, pernicious. Intelligence, ability, motive, perception, reaction, temperament, habit, and
all other factors at this level are, from the vantage point of a higher level,
simply material which, along with material as solid as wood and stone,
has to be molded to higher service. There is, of course, a psychology of
morals, but sociology, if one is driven to putting it thus, is about the
morality in morals. It is because of considerations like those just presented that sociologists say that social structures can be described without
reference to the particularity of individuals. It will have created misunderstanding if anyone has claimed "without reference to individuals."
Individuals are always there, but one individual with the standard qualifications will do as well as another. The individuals can be changed and
the structure remain constant. The committee changes hands but its
name, offices, and work continue as before. There is *replaceability of incumbents*. And this concludes the list of fifteen properties of conduct

I wished to draw attention to in support of its superindividuality. Diagram 8 gives a summary of them.

Diagram 8

Indicators of the

Superindividuality of Individual Conduct

1. Coactivity in differentiated roles
   ("organic" solidarity by division of labor)

2. Shared expectation ("mechanical" solidarity
   by moral consensus, "collective conscience")

3. Exteriority of norms to the person   } Durkheim's five

4. Constraint through sanctions

5. Standardization of practice

6. Continuance of association

7. Continuing supply of product

8. Identity of the activity

9. Resonance of social action

10. "Reproduction"

11. Equipment mediating interaction

12. Hierarchical ordering   (a) of actions
                             (b) of roles
                             (c) of equipment

13. Symbolization of activity

14. Transmissibility of cultural symbols

15. Replaceability of incumbents

It is more or less arbitrary, incidentally, how one goes about this kind of defense. Loomis's work presents such a defense in effect, when he introduces what he calls a "processually articulated structural model" of the social system and identifies nine elements in it.[52] These are all paralleled in one or more of my fifteen items, except possibly for one. Loomis's shorter list, however, scarcely covers everything present in mine. Loomis catalogues knowledge, sentiment, end, norms, mastery of skills for status-roles, ranking, acceptance of authority and power, rewards and penalties for motivation, and facilities. Sentiment is the one not closely paralleled in my list of items. This of course only constitutes an element of a social system if we are considering the mutuality or otherwise of sentiments with regard to an activity or to the norms and values that guide it. Sentiment

[52] C. P. Loomis, *Social Systems, Essays on Their Persistence and Change* (Princeton: D. Van Nostrand Co., Inc., 1960).

then is a centrifugal or centripetal social force. Probably most of what
Loomis intends by *sentiment* would be taken care of by *shared expectation,* for the latter involves affective and moral elements.

Although the foregoing suggests that organization and a certain
stability are inherent in the definition of society itself, this of course does
not require that society be unchanging. The stability of structures rests
on a continuing and pervasive shared expectation among those who uphold them, however this be achieved: it may be achieved through passive
acquiescence or even, in the extreme case, through coercion. (It may be
worth remembering, too, that it can be an expectation of continuing hos-
tilities as much as of anything else. It is naïve to assume that conflict
excludes shared expectation: if conflict is to be continuing, it soon becomes institutionalized.) But this consensus is always shifting somewhat
and liable to eruption. For this reason, collective behavior in such manifestations as crowds, revivals, rumors, revolts, public opinion, fashions,
and movements is rightly taken by sociologists to be a superindividual
thing, and thus an ingredient of society. Durkheim named them well, for
you might say they are "currents" in the interstitial social fluids, providing the solvents out of which the more precise definition of social structures crystallizes and into which it may again dissolve. We only have a
sociological appreciation of them if we see them thus, as influences which
erode more permanent forms and shore them up again. Manifestations
of collective behavior might be thought of as social structure stretched
out and attenuated almost to breaking point, but still not snapping: the
tie that persists is the intensified belief-sharing. Another way of putting it
might be to say that these are manifestations of disturbance in the social
unconscious—if in speaking thus of an unconscious we refer purely metaphorically to the shared strivings toward a consensus of attitude and perception which people in association always make, even though much of it
is unconscious to themselves.

Yet, although we speak only metaphorically in referring thus to a
social unconscious, we are touching on something which exists in its own
right. It is not a group "mind" certainly, but it is just as certainly a group
reality. Has not McDougall's notion been glibly dismissed with too much
attention to his form of words and too little attention to the substance
behind them? [53] Newcomb, in reporting recently on his own work on
consensus, was mainly concerned, as a social psychologist, with the psychological processes involved in achieving this state.[54] But he sets forth, as

[53] W. McDougall, *The Group Mind: A Sketch of the Principles of Collective Psychology, With Some Attempt to Apply Them to the Interpretation of National Life
and Character* (Cambridge: The University Press, 1927).
[54] T. M. Newcomb, "The Study of Consensus," in *Sociology Today: Problems and
Prospects,* ed. Merton, Broom, and Cottrell, pp. 277–92.

one of his justifications for studying it, his belief that social consensus is an important sociological phenomenon in its own right. He accepts the view that it is the necessary condition of social organization, and explicitly endorses in doing so the various views developed in this connection by Comte, Park and Burgess, Tarde, Le Bon, Durkheim, Cooley, and Mead.

There has been a certain tendency to think that collective behavior is a softer edge of sociology and "more psychological." But it is more correct to say there are both psychological and sociological aspects to it, just as is the case with the study of socialization. The same is no less true, for that matter, of the study of organizational structure, for there is a psychology of people in roles. (Diagram 9 suggests how each discipline makes its claim on these areas of study.) Because the mental states of people caught up in collective episodes are so interesting, it is possible they may receive greater attention. The Langs' study of collective behavior gives just about equal attention to both the sociological and psy-

Areas of Study Having Both

Psychological and Sociological Aspects

Diagram 9

Sociology of . . .	Socialization	Organization	Collective behavior
Psychology of . . .	Socialization	Organization	Collective behavior

chological aspects, and this is one possible way of attacking the subject.[55] But the sociological approach of course is concerned with what is "collective" in collective behavior. In what sense collective behavior connects with more solid social structure, and makes a transition between successive states of it, is a fundamental question of sociology. Smelser's study addresses this.[56] As mentioned earlier, Smelser suggests that the various kinds of collective behavior reconstitute some component of action that has been impaired. Behavior directed by hysterical and wish-fulfilment beliefs reconstitutes facilities. That which is directed by hostile beliefs reconstitutes both facilities and the mobilization of motivation for role performance. Behavior directed by norm-oriented beliefs reconstitutes norms, that directed by value-oriented beliefs values. I am not able to make quite the same approach as Smelser to the array of material he uses. I want to rotate it on its axis. Possibly because I think of values themselves somewhat differently, it seems to me better to view *all* collective behavior as the reaffirmation of some value. It is like a declaration that some satis-

[55] K. Lang and G. E. Lang, *Collective Dynamics* (New York: Thomas Y. Crowell Co., Inc., 1963).
[56] N. Smelser, *Theory of Collective Behavior* (New York: The Free Press of Glencoe, Inc., 1962).

faction or other is worthy as an end in itself and is therefore a justification
for social cohesion in the pursuit of it. After structural breakdown men
are seeking a new rallying point to come together. Thus in collective
behavior, separated men try to erect the keystone for a social structure
worthy of their renewed devotion. It may fall out and be tried again and
again before it effectively closes an arch over them. Because there is more
zeal than knowledge in the act, it may never do so. It is at any rate a
hopeful gesture. Elsewhere I have argued that there are five ends men
can make self-sufficient; that is to say, there are five available values.[57]
These are membership, partisanship, ownership, interest, and face. Typi-
cally, social movements seek to reconstitute membership and partisanship,
hysterical and wish-fulfilment beliefs seek to reconstitute ownership, hostile outbursts to reconstitute partisanship, crazes interest, fads and fashions face.

As a conclusion to this chapter, a word can be said about the *synthesist* idea of sociology. It has two variants, although the first of them is
almost nonexistent now. This was the idea that sociology is a kind of
synthesis of all knowledge, including the natural sciences. It was something like this conception that Lester Ward advanced in his *Dynamic
Sociology*.[58] In a manner reminiscent of the synthetic philosophy of
Herbert Spencer,[59] and in part modeled after it, he aimed to trace the
operation of one principle at successively higher levels in the evolution
and ultimate constitution of society. Society, Ward proposed, is the final
result of a great cosmic process of aggregation, the forming of compounds
from simpler components. The process leads back to the material atom
as its source. Presumably Ward derived this notion from the idea that
society was the highest level of reality which science should investigate
and that, insofar as all lower levels are compounded into the higher,
society included everything. There is a certain amount of sense in this,
but it could nevertheless lead to a misunderstanding. For it might be
taken to imply that no statement about a higher-order reality can stand
on its own, but that all the lower-order factors underlying it must be
explicitly spelled out. Yet, as a trial in the perennial quest to synthesize
all knowledge, Ward's approach has something to commend it, and it will
doubtless find its champions again. Were any such synthesis ever worked
out, however, it would clearly not be a sociology.

[57] H. Fallding, "A Proposal for the Empirical Study of Values," *American Sociological Review*, **30** (1965), 223–33.

[58] L. F. Ward, *Dynamic Sociology, or Applied Social Science as Based Upon Statistical Sociology and the Less Complex Sciences* (New York: Appleton-Century-Crofts,
Inc., 1883).

[59] H. Spencer, *A System of Synthetic Philosophy* (London: Williams & Norgate,
1870–1896).

The other synthesist view is that sociology is the synthesis of all the social sciences: demography, social and cultural anthropology, social psychology, economics, political science (and, of course, sociology itself). But if sociology does have any synthesizing influence among the social sciences, it could only be because it provides the concepts basic to them. They would then, in fact, be branches of sociology whether their exponents know it or not. It may be profitable to ask whether this is in fact true.

I have argued that neither demography nor any social psychology that is rightly so called is a branch of sociology. On the other hand, cultural and social anthropology comprise nothing more nor less than the sociology of the simpler peoples, so I think one is entitled to claim all of it for sociology. I confess to being completely stumped, however, by the importance of urging any distinction between cultural and social anthropology. But I assume that the recent stress on *social* in British anthropology is an announcement that the sociological point of view of Durkheim, Radcliffe-Brown, and Malinowski has prevailed over any mere collector's interest in the works of man. As for economics, the study of economic institutions is, of course, a part of sociology. Yet sociology is only concerned with the organization of economic activity, and cannot evaluate it economically, which is precisely what economics sets out to do. Although there is a close complementarity, then, economics seems to have a subject matter which is distinct. For the natural resources and artificial commodities that lie under man's influence have relations among themselves that affect their value. Economists have recently shown much deference to (what they call) the noneconomic factors in (what they call) economic behavior, and thereby acknowledge a certain dependence on sociological data. This seems to be largely a recognition that the values of the society as a whole will affect the differential demand for goods and services within it, so that an economy cannot be studied realistically unless these constraints are known.

The situation with regard to political science is rather different. Insofar as this is science and not simply a commentary on affairs or a training in administration, political science must be viewed as a branch of sociology. Lipset states that political science has been distinguished from political sociology in practice simply by concentrating attention on the state, whereas the latter regards the state in the context of other institutions having some political bearing, which ramify through the society.[60] The former has consequently stressed efficiency in public administration, the latter the possible stresses and strains of bureaucracy, and general social conflict and change. Be that as it may, as I have stressed, we are concerned here with definition from principles, and different emphases in practice

[60] S. M. Lipset, "Political Sociology," in *Sociology Today, Problems and Prospects,* ed. Merton, Broom, and Cottrell, pp. 81–114.

can scarcely be allowed to divert us. The intellectual problems of political science have to do with the consolidation of power and its forms of legitimation. They entail questions about the achievement of consensus, the building of political organization upon it, and the socialization of citizens in the resulting system. This is all sociology, and insofar as sociological resources are utilized political scientists might expect to be the more scientific. Of course, political science is a field of study in its own right, even if, systematically considered, it makes but a branch of sociology. It is easily the oldest field of study in social science; and there are plenty of political systems to study and a vast literature to master.

Let me repeat why it has seemed important to make so many seemingly invidious distinctions: It is not to drive a wedge between the branches of social science, but to further the distinctive contribution of each. If anyone is imbued with a passion to bring unity into the social sciences, he may be assured that obliterating their distinctness will not help. Unity is a harmony of differentiated parts, and we will approach it more closely as we approach a clearer differentiation. There is no unity at all in confusion. I have claimed that it falls to sociology to account for social systems, and in the following chapter I show what intellectual burdens must be assumed and risks taken to succeed in this enterprise.

chapter 6

Characterizing Value Judgments
as Judgments of Fact
Regarding Function

The idea reigns that to see societies and their cultures objectively you must shun ideology. Even worse: Since student days many have borne the reproach of being handicapped sociologists because they were committed citizens, holding certain convictions dear. It was by innuendo more than by plain speech that we were told this. But there was a vulgar victimization in all this and an assuming ignorance. Two fallacies were being handed sticks to beat us with.

The first is the fallacy that sets judgments of value and judgments of fact wholly apart; whereas it is value *commitments* that differ from intellectual judgments of fact. There is a class of intellectual judgments of fact that are judgments of value in the purely intellectual sense of *judgment*. These judgments simply make the observation that, in terms of its nature, something is good or bad, and they do not add anything by way of personal preference or exhortation to others to side for or against the phenomenon reported. You can use your intellect to judge whether a cabbage, a lung, a piano, a bridge, a surgeon, a marriage, or a constitution is good or bad, and still leave entirely unsaid what attitude you mean to take to the fact. If a line is to be drawn in discussions about value it is here. Yet most commonly the line has been drawn elsewhere. Encouragingly, the thaw on this great misunderstanding has apparently begun.

In 1961, in *The Structure of Science,* Nagel asked us to distinguish between "characterizing value judgments," which are simply descriptive, and "appraising value judgments," which convey a commitment.[1] He went on to say:

[1] E. Nagel, *The Structure of Science: Problems in the Logic of Scientific Explanation* (New York: Harcourt, Brace & World, Inc., 1961), pp. 485–502.

It is clear . . . that an investigator making a characterizing value
judgment is not thereby logically bound to affirm or deny a corresponding appraising evaluation. It is no less evident that he
cannot consistently make an appraising value judgment about a
given instance (e.g., that it is undesirable for a given animal to
continue being anemic), unless he can affirm a characterizing
judgment about that instance independently of the appraising
one (e.g., that the animal is anemic). Accordingly, although characterizing judgments are necessarily entailed by many appraising
judgments, making appraising judgments is not a necessary condition for making characterizing ones.[2]

We may profitably note another point to which Nagel here draws
attention. It is just because the world of our experience presents us with
objects that can be characterized as good or bad that we deem it appropriate to make decisions for or against things. We are not indignant over
his prejudices if a cook decides to throw out a bad cabbage or if a patient
decides no longer to call on a bad surgeon and advises his friends to do
the same. On the contrary, we think these decisions show "good judgment." Nothing could be more naïve, then, than to suppose that value
commitments originate quite spontaneously, removed from knowledge of
the existing situation. Nothing could be more perverse, either, than to
condemn them as arising from prejudices when they are unflattering to
ourselves and to excuse them when they are not. If they are no threat
to us, they are likely to be excused as capricious expressions of personal
whim in which anyone is entitled to follow his inclination unchecked—
because there are no checks that can be applied.

An ideology is simply a case of this object-based commitment. It is a
two-stranded thing, in which there is an intellectual judgment about the
social structure that can be separated from pleas to take action about it.
The intellectual component of ideologies may be more or less informed,
yet it makes a folk or layman's or rule-of-thumb sociology. To locate
oneself as a sociologist, then, one should, rather than shun ideology, ap-
preciate its kinship with the science of sociology while being sophisticated
about its pleading. We have come to sociology by asking the questions
that ideology reckons with, not by backing away from them.

The second fallacy that was allowed to victimize us was the other side
of the same coin, yet it was something more than the failure to distinguish intellectual judgment from commitment. It was the fixed idea that
an objective study of society would not yield intellectual judgments of
value as its fruit—what Nagel calls *characterizing value judgments*. Propositions having this appearance must be intruders: philosophy or theology

[2] *Ibid.*, p. 493. Reprinted by permission of the publisher.

or something of that kind, not science. Positive science, so the refrain went, simply reports on relationships. Relationships *between what* is a question it was not thought important to explore. Yet this glib image of social science forces questions closed that are still entirely open and does so in an assuming way. For there is a distinguished tradition at least as old as Aristotle that thinks altogether otherwise, and which has never been effectively challenged. Aron describes it very succinctly when locating Alexis de Tocqueville within it:

> Tocqueville, therefore, was a sociologist who never ceased to judge while he described. In this sense, he belonged to the tradition of classical political philosophers who would not have conceived of analyzing regimes without judging them at the same time.
>
> If I have emphasized the links between Tocqueville and Montesquieu, I have also suggested the links between Montesquieu and Aristotle. In the history of sociology, Tocqueville remains closest to classical philosophy, as interpreted by Prof. Leo Strauss.
>
> In Aristotle's eyes, one cannot interpret tyranny correctly unless one sees it as the regime furthest removed from the best of regimes, for the reality of the fact is inseparable from the quality of this fact. To try to describe institutions without judging them is to miss what constitutes them as such. Tocqueville remained in this tradition. His description of the United States was also an explanation of the means by which freedom is safeguarded in a democratic society, and it reveals throughout what threatens the equilibrium of American society. This very language implies a judgment, and Tocqueville did not believe he was violating the rules of social science by judging in and by his description. If he had been questioned, he would probably have replied (perhaps like Montesquieu, or in any case like Aristotle), that a description cannot be faithful unless it includes those judgments intrinsically related to the description, since in fact a regime is what it is by its own quality, and a tyranny can only be described as a tyranny.[3]

The avowed functionalists in sociology, as well as the unavowed when they take a functionalist stance, which they do often, must be considered the inheritors of this tradition whether they are aware of it or not. It is curious in what a diversity of things both the defenders and detractors of functionalism have considered its essence to lie. *In my view it lies in this*. It was substantially this "value" position that Nadel expounded, for

[3] From *Main Currents in Sociological Thought* by Raymond Aron (Basic Books, Inc., New York, 1965).

instance, and Emmet endorsed and elaborated.[4] I would stand with it. For I assume that in generating social organization and a culture to protect it, societies and their component subgroups are always striving, consciously or unconsciously, for specifiable qualities of corporate life that may or may not be attained. To measure the degree of attainment is to make objective scientific measurement of the dimensions intrinsic in human association: it is at the same time to evaluate and judge. In succeeding chapters, it will be my aim to suggest what these desiderata might be, thereby eliciting specific dimensions of functional measurement of the kind Hempel has asked for.[5] I will do this for both culture and social organization, for there is no virtue in studying one without taking the other into account: their combined study makes one discipline of sociology in the classical, comprehensive sense. The tendency to make organization the province of sociology and culture that of anthropology seems obtuse and petty. Furthermore, as the negatives of these dimensions are explored, the way in which disorganization is implicated in dysfunction will begin to appear plainer. The kinship between these two chief mourners has scarcely yet been traced.

It is my belief that a unified sociology will only come into being when the dimensions of measurement named in the chapters to follow, or something like them, are applied to all the separate substantive fields of sociological investigation. Nor am I proposing any tender-minded, non-scientific sociology. I am laboring on the groundwork of a completely hardheaded science. Whether there can be a value-free sociology is a question that can be unequivocally answered, and it is answered by splitting the question in two. Sociology can be free from *appraising* value judgments, but *characterizing* value judgments are in its blood. If in mistaken zeal we tried to purge sociology of characterizing value judgments, we would keep nothing worth knowing. At the same time, *as sociologists,* we are only entitled to report on matters of value descriptively. We can and should exclude expressions of choice. Sociology is for understanding the world; no authority arises from it for changing the world. It is quite possible we will want to use our sociological knowledge to further the ends to which we are committed on other grounds. There can be no objection to that when we step out of the academic role. But we need to be aware that, when we apply sociology, we are not engaged in furthering the science: we are furthering *by* science the political, commercial, religious, philanthropic, or other practical causes we happen to favor. Sociology

4 S. F. Nadel, *Anthropology and Modern Life* (Canberra: Australian National University, 1953). D. Emmet, *Function, Purpose and Powers* (London: Macmillan & Company, Ltd., 1958).

5 C. G. Hempel, "The Logic of Functional Analysis," in *Symposium on Sociological Theory,* ed. L. Gross (Evanston, Illinois: Row, Peterson & Co., 1959), pp. 271–307.

could possibly be called a normative science, but only if the split I am insisting on is observed. It cannot say what anyone ought to do, in the sense of giving authorization for action. It can say whether action taken was, or will be, beneficial.

Sociology treats behavior in situations that pose a problem of regulation, rather than dealing solely with situations where regulation is achieved. But before we ever speak of social events, a system of regulated interpersonal contact either exists in some degree, or the participants are aware that one is called for and have adumbrated it—or, having lost what was won, have abrogated it. To designate the realized desideratum we can speak of a *group* or, alternatively, of *social arrangements, social organization, social structure, social system. Social system* is perhaps preferable to *group,* for common speech seems to imply a set of people by the term *group,* whereas we only mean to refer to the segments of people that are surrendered to a common activity. If in this book *group* is used more or less interchangeably with *social system, group* will be understood to have this more precise meaning. If one speaks of the functions of a social system as a whole, it is simply to specify what products are secured through the bridges and bonds thus established between man and man. It may be bread or bullion, music or medicine, sympathy or salvation. Then if one speaks in addition of the function of any activity *contained within* a social system, one refers to the effect it has in strengthening (or weakening) these productive bonds. For instance, Coser has analyzed conflict as having positive functions in some social structures, and by this he simply means that it can strengthen existing productive bonds by sealing their corrosions—e.g., when a hampering grievance is aired and removed and everyone is "able to get on with the job." [6] Contained within a casket of existing bonds, conflict may work like fire to purge them of imperfections; but, without these, it would presumably not even constitute a social phenomenon, much less a functional one.

The notion of *function* in connection with societies and their component groups has been variously employed, as Merton showed.[7] But the usage that has come to prevail takes as the function of an activity *within a system* the contribution it makes to the whole. We have therefore come to see the importance of specifying precisely both the part and the whole to which a functional statement refers. A practice which is functional within one social region need not be functional in one which is more (or less) inclusive. Other things also have to be specified if functional statements are to mean anything. As Nagel stressed, we should say to what

[6] L. A. Coser, *The Functions of Social Conflict* (New York: The Free Press of Glencoe, Inc., 1956).
[7] R. K. Merton, "Manifest and Latent Functions," in *Social Theory and Social Structure* (New York: The Free Press of Glencoe, Inc., 1957), pp. 19–84.

state of the whole the practice in question is contributory (he designates such a system state *G*).[8] But, just as important as any of this, should we not bear in mind all the time what the product of the whole system is, as this itself may or may not be functional for those who bear the cost of the system and so expect to benefit? Very frequently in sociology it is whole, bounded action-systems that are being judged to be functional or dysfunctional *for man* and, only by transference, any parts within them which may make them so. And this is because social action is prompted by human need.

The examination of the properties of the *functional system* that has been undertaken by Nagel seems to concentrate on the penultimate question of the sustained functioning of the system of action and does not ask whether, when functioning, it is functional for those who operate it.[9] Nagel's formalization greatly facilitates our analysis of the internal processes of change and compensatory counterchange by which a system preserves equilibrium.[10] But this has to be linked to the ultimate question of whether the system itself is functional or dysfunctional in yielding products matched to human need. In my view, asking this ultimate question is what makes it worthwhile to ask the penultimate one. Malinowski's insistence on this is one of his enduring contributions to the discussion.[11]

Furthermore, there is a teleological residue in functional thinking that is scarcely disposed of by Nagel's demonstration that the explanatory element in functionalism is simply causal explanation put in a roundabout way.[12] Where a system state or need-satisfaction stands at the end of a process of human endeavor, it exercises some directive power over the efforts taken to achieve it. Here we have a case, then, of the kind of process for which Braithwaite has striven to preserve recognition, wherein the anticipated future goal controls the present movement toward it, so that the end achieved is not the passive effect of a causal chain but, in a certain sense at least, the cause of its own causes.[13] Braithwaite points out that the field of study explored by cybernetics is largely concerned with teleological mechanisms like this. Such processes, once launched, may achieve the end in view—or may fail and so be "in vain." Does not the anticipation of an end to be achieved underlie all our judgments of function or dysfunction, when those judgments are made in such a way as to imply a comparison with the alternative possible outcome? It seems to me that

---

8 E. Nagel, "A Formalization of Functionalism," in *Logic Without Metaphysics* (New York: The Free Press of Glencoe, Inc., 1956), pp. 247–83.

9 *Ibid.*

10 *Ibid.*

11 B. Malinowski, *A Scientific Theory of Culture, and Other Essays* (New York: Oxford University Press, 1960).

12 Nagel, "A Formalization of Functionalism."

13 R. B. Braithwaite, *Scientific Explanation, a Study of the Function of Theory, Probability and Law in Science* (Cambridge: The University Press, 1959), pp. 319–41.

what we are interested in *when we make this comparison* is not explanation but evaluation.

We assume that group endeavor is constrained by system states and need-satisfactions, regardless of the extent to which the actors formulate these as aims. It is out of the collectivity itself that these pressures spring, and they only become aims in the minds of the actors as these discern the demands implicit in their situation. Merton distinguished *manifest* from *latent* functions, the former being those effects that the actors actually intend.[14] This can be a useful distinction for some purposes, but there is a sense in which it must be ignored in a natural science of society. In such a science we seek to trace the effects of action, and it is all one whether they were intended or not. It may be important to recognize an intention among the causes of an effect, but the effect will not be functional or dysfunctional in any different way through being intended or not.

Functional analysis became unpopular in some quarters because of the phrase *functional explanation*. This seemed to imply not only that *functionalism* was a method of explanation but a special one. But I have referred to Nagel's point that the explanation in functional statements is the same as in any other, except that it takes an inverted expression.[15] I would deny that the special importance of *functionalism* ever lay in its gift for explaining. It lay rather in showing that we are dealing with operating systems in sociology. It was thus an early signpost to relevant measurement and belongs to the natural history phase of the science. Another reason for the unpopularity of *functionalism* with some scholars, especially some trained in anthropology, was that they lingered too long beating the dead horse of Malinowskian functionalism. Malinowski developed his perception of systems by supposing that if any practice was kept up over time it must be because it had a positive function for the group.[16] Because the function was not always self-evident, it could become a sign of sociological acumen to guess what it was. Only recently Whitaker has written a critique of functionalism taking that for his definition of it.[17]

14 Merton, *op. cit.*

15 Nagel, "A Formalization of Functionalism."

16 B. Malinowski, *The Sexual Life of Savages in North-Western Melanesia*, 3rd ed., with Special Foreword (London: Routledge & Kegan Paul, Ltd., 1932); "Culture," *Encyclopaedia of the Social Sciences* (New York: The Macmillan Company, 1937); *The Dynamics of Culture Change, An Inquiry into Race Relations in Africa* (New Haven: Yale University Press, 1945); *Argonauts of the Western Pacific, An Account of Native Enterprise and Adventure in the Archipelagoes of Melanesian New Guinea* (New York: E. P. Dutton & Co., Inc., 1953); and *A Scientific Theory of Culture, and Other Essays* (New York: Oxford University Press, 1960).

17 I. Whitaker, "The Nature and Value of Functionalism in Sociology," in *Functionalism in the Social Sciences: The Strength and Limits of Functionalism in Anthropology, Economics, Political Science and Sociology*. Monograph 5 in a series sponsored by the American Academy of Political and Social Science, ed. D. Martindale (Philadelphia, Feb. 1965), 127–43.

But Bales and Parsons leapt far beyond this when they suggested that any group will have certain functional imperatives and the practices it sanctions may or may not serve to fulfil them.[18] This allowed the possibility of judging whether a customary practice was "functional" or whether, indeed, it may even be "dysfunctional."

Functional analysis, through its *functional imperatives,* introduced into sociology the criterion variable or goal state of feedback systems. They are the same, also, as Hempel's dimensions of functional measurement and Nagel's *G*'s. Without having the benefit of more recent cybernetic thought, Bales and Parsons have proved extremely far-seeing in this. These "imperatives" have seemed almost ludicrous to some of their readers—slippery, not-very-empirical things. The social system "needed" them but didn't necessarily have them, yet tended toward them because it "needed" them. What could this double-talk mean? Yet when states like adaptation or integration were designated system imperatives, what was being implied was that deviations from them might sometimes work to correct themselves. Oscillations about these points were what gave concern to people in groups.

Parsons shows a developing understanding of the functional imperatives in his published work, but has given a consolidated statement on them in *Theories of Society.*[19] He sees four imperatives in groups; that is, four states have to be realized for them to be effective. There is *pattern maintenance and tension reduction:* respect for the whole sanctioning of the group's efforts must be preserved against attrition and incidental demoralization. There is *goal attainment:* the group must be decisive about its priorities and persevere in them. There is *adaptation:* the group must equip itself to endure and operate in its situation. Finally, there is *integration:* its diverse activities must cohere and be unified. In this book I do not adopt Parsons' functional imperatives exactly as he gave them. But those I adopt resemble his closely, and when I refer to *functionalism* in general, it is to *functionalism* as Parsons developed it that I make reference. This seems to be the meaning given to it now in sociology. Yet its radical implications have scarcely been faced yet. It is essentially a recognition that groups are artifacts that will need to be built aright, and it amounts to a method of measurement by evaluating their performance. (However, let me not be misunderstood when I say this. This is not the

18 R. F. Bales, *Interaction Process Analysis, A Method for the Study of Small Groups* (Cambridge, Massachusetts: Addison-Wesley Publishing Company, Inc., 1951). T. Parsons, "An Outline of the Social System," in *Theories of Society: Foundations of Modern Sociological Theory,* ed. T. Parsons, E. Shils, K. D. Naegele, and J. R. Pitts (New York: The Free Press of Glencoe, Inc., 1962), pp. 30–79.

19 *Ibid.*; C. Morse, "The Functional Imperatives," in *The Social Theories of Talcott Parsons,* ed. Max Black (Englewood Cliffs, N.J.: Prentice-Hall, Inc., 1962), pp. 100–152.

kind of evaluation sometimes attempted in what are called "evaluation studies," where the sociologist undertakes to measure how successful some group is in accomplishing its aims. The functional perspective gives us the means by which to evaluate the group's aims in terms of its existence also. Unless we stand outside on our own platform and measure what we choose, it is doubtful that our measurements will make a contribution to science. Sociologists must keep the privileges of the *deus ex machina* or suffocate.)

This characterizing evaluation in functional analysis is objective and needs no apology. To ask for the function of any social arrangement is to call for its justification—or alternatively for its condemnation. The positive-negative polarity inherent in the terms *(eu)functional* and *dysfunctional* should betray at once that this evaluation is afoot. A great deal of unnecessary hedging in sociological work would be obviated if this could be frankly admitted. At the same time, sociological work could be more easily purged of covert, private evaluations if it were allowed that evaluation of this objective kind is intrinsic in sociological analysis, and altogether honorable. Yet, in saying this, we have to distinguish between the two meanings given to *subjective* when that state of mind is unfavorably contrasted with the *objective*. It can mean "biased" *or* "intuitive." When it has the former meaning, *subjectivity* is to be deplored, because the observer's perception is distorted by it. When it has the latter meaning it is simply to be regretted, for the observer is not yet able to share his vision of what may well be the truth. The first kind of subjectivity has to be expunged from science, but the second kind is the *anlage* of science and has to be protected and fostered until its testimony can be objectified. In saying that the evaluation in functional analysis is objective, freedom from subjectivity of the first kind is mainly what is being claimed, of course. Yet we may hope that freedom from subjectivity of the second kind can also be achieved with time.

We imply objective evaluation of two kinds, in fact, whenever we specify a function. Basically, we are making a judgment as to whether the expenditure that goes into the creation and maintenance of the arrangement is worthwhile; but we determine this worthwhileness by both a backward and a forward look, as it were. The backward look tries to sum up the efficiency of the arrangement in producing its effects. To the extent that it is inefficient, wasteful, it is dysfunctional in a way. The forward look examines whether the effects themselves are valuable in terms of some schedule of needs which we postulate for the life of man in society. Some instances will make this plainer.

We may say, as Gluckman has done, that the function of rituals of rebellion in Africa is to channel off the resentment that the natives feel for their chiefs and so preserve stability in the existing authority arrangements—thereby ensuring the continuing supply of everything those arrangements guarantee.[20] We would then be implying (1) that these ritual expressions of aggression are efficient means of dissipating resentment and so preserving stability; and (2) that a society needs to maintain an uninterrupted need-satisfaction by having stability. We may say, with Davis and Moore, that the function of social stratification is to "insure that the most important positions are conscientiously filled by the most qualified persons." [21] We would then be implying (1) that a grading of rewards is an efficient means of motivating suitable persons to accept greater responsibilities, while a division of labor into tasks of unequal importance is an efficient means of stabilizing the work organization; and (2) that a stable work organization is necessary to satisfy common needs continuously. We may say, with Merton,[22] that the function of the political boss in the U.S. is "to organize, centralize and maintain in good working condition 'the scattered fragments of power' which are at present dispersed." [23] We would then be implying (1) that buying political support from diversified groups by dispensing help to them is an efficient means of concentrating power, while all such groups need some access to power and the power secured by them needs to be concentrated to achieve stability; and (2) that stability assures the flow of need-satisfactions. Or finally we may say, with Parsons, that two functions of institutionalizing a "collectivity-orientation" in the professional role of the scientist are (a) to protect the public from arbitrary interference by men whose special knowledge gives them an advantage, and (b) to expose the ideas of any scientist to the critical scrutiny of his fellows.[24] We would then be implying (1) that this kind of role-institutionalization is an efficient means of restraining individuals who, in an intellectual sense, handle dynamite, so that their contribution to knowledge can be utilized for adaptive social change; and (2) that a failure to make adaptive changes blocks the satisfaction of needs.

Perhaps it would save misunderstanding if the reader appreciated that evaluations made in the above manner are sociological evaluations only. *So far as present society is concerned,* X *is functional,* Y *dysfunctional*—that is always the implicit stipulation. There may well be supernal heights or historical perspectives from which a socially functional arrangement can be judged bad and a dysfunctional one good—just as ill health is sometimes recalled with gratitude because it brought spiritual

20 M. Gluckman, *Rituals of Rebellion in South-East Africa* (Manchester: University of Manchester Press, 1954).

21 K. Davis and W. E. Moore, "Some Principles of Stratification," *American Sociological Review,* **10** (1945), 242–49 (quote is on 243). See also K. Davis, *Human Society* (New York: The Macmillian Company, 1959), pp. 364–89.

22 Merton, *op. cit.,* pp. 70–82.

23 *Ibid.,* p. 72.

24 T. Parsons, *The Social System* (London: Tavistock, 1952), pp. 335–45.

blessing, or poverty because it put one in the way of great fortune at a later time. But that would not be incompatible with recognizing the arrangements as *socially* functional or dysfunctional. Merton makes this same point when he insists that judgments about social disorganization are not moralizing judgments but technical judgments about the working of social systems.[25] Furthermore, this helps us to see why intellectual judgments about function and dysfunction contain no ethical imperative. We cannot pass from "The instruction of children is functional" to "Thou shalt instruct children." As sociologists we hold no whip. (Fortunately, though, our sociology is redeemed from the final futility by the fact that men exist who are not merely sociologists.)

Another point, about the disputed notion of *social pathology:* Evaluating social arrangements as functional or dysfunctional is equivalent to classifying them as normal or pathological. This is a necessary preliminary to the search for causal explanation. A physiologist cannot discover the function of the liver by generalizing directly from a random collection of livers which contains some diseased specimens. He distinguishes between the diseased and healthy organs at the outset and, setting the diseased ones aside, generalizes from the healthy ones. Certainly, *by contrast*, he gains some understanding of healthy functioning from an examination of the diseased cases, but he can only do so if he first sets them in opposition by classifying them apart. His account of the liver would be altogether confounded if it simply averaged the properties of the whole collection. Distinguishing normal from pathological cases is one of his *first* tasks, and precedes causal knowledge of the conditions of normal or pathological functioning. Social systems are more complex than livers, of course, but the two things are alike in this respect. The above instance therefore serves to show the confusion that can invade an intellectual discipline concerned with things that have system-properties if it fails to recognize that character in them and evaluate them accordingly. It shows further, why evaluation, forced upon us in this way, is simply *scientific measurement*. It amounts to quantification of those dynamic properties the possession of which defines the class of things in question. To evaluate systems is to have appropriated the dimensions for measuring them. It also suggests to us a homelier approach to social pathology. We begin to see that this scarcely constitutes a field of study in its own right, but refers to a kind of negative possibility extending through all social life. If we are to become scientific measurers by habit, it will have to be our pre-

25 R. K. Merton, "Social Problems and Sociological Theory," in *Contemporary Social Problems, An Introduction to the Sociology of Deviant Behavior and Social Disorganization,* ed. R. K. Merton and R. A. Nisbet (New York: Harcourt, Brace & World, Inc., 1961), pp. 719–23.

occupation to ask how sociologically healthy—or pathological—is any occurrence whatever.

It may require a titanic effort to overcome the clinging prejudice that *any* view about social desiderata will be ideologically colored and therefore suspect, but the effort has to be made. Throughout the whole of modern sociology, certain objective imperatives have been fulminating, forcing recognition for themselves. To illustrate the point we will have to anticipate part of a later chapter: For instance, *both* adaptive change (which implies rationality) and stability have usually been assumed necessary in the social arrangements men make. These are two of the components of efficiency which, it was said, we gauge by a kind of backward look. They are states of the social system (Nagel's *G*'s) without which the system cannot be properly productive of anything. They are, as such, nobody's political ideology; and there is no sense in calling a sociologist conservative or radical because his work illustrates the necessity of the one or the other —as likely as not it will illustrate the necessity of both. Man, an anxious creature who looks before and after, works for his satisfactions over time and has therefore to bind time; social organization and culture take their origin from this and must therefore develop a certain conservatism to be of service to him. Yet, even in its most colloquial usage, *stability* has never meant *fixity:* we must not suppose that stable social arrangements are arrangements that are fixed forever. They are simply arrangements that materialize as expected for as long as they are wanted. In no sense, either, is stability the *opposite* of change; so it would be wrong to think that combining them necessarily means striking some mean of moderation or gradualism. Commitment to stability still leaves men free to adapt to a world which changes, or of which their knowledge changes, by various means. To be of service, stable social arrangements must yield—they must have a certain plasticity.

We have no choice, then, except to take as normal, healthy, or functional those social arrangements that exhibit both stability and adaptive change in the combination demanded by the time and place, and as abnormal, pathological or dysfunctional in some degree those that do not (and this is of course a matter of degree). It is admittedly a delicate calculation to make—often still largely beyond us—so we make it in a rough, rule-of-thumb way (perhaps in a way which is subjective in the second of the above senses). Yet make it we must—and early in the sorting of our data. Thus are arrangements classified sociologically: one set of arrangements is given a negative sociological valency so that it will not be confused with the positive counterpart which in other respects deceptively resembles it. The well-organized family is thus not to be taken for the same sociological phenomenon as the disorganized one, the high-morale department store for the same thing as the low-morale store, the nation riddled with suicide and homicide for the same thing as the one where these are rare, the church or school which moves with the times for the same thing as the one made redundant through its archaisms. Martindale states that all the critics of the notion of social disorganization base their objection at least partly on the fact that evaluations are inherent in it.[26] Could the critics see that the need for evaluations originates from the data and not from the evaluators, the practice might seem less objectionable to them. It is only after we have set contrasting phenomena in classes apart that we can sample the cases in each class and arrive at causal laws about functional and dysfunctional systems. It would be a pity if the attention that has been given to functionalism were taken for an invitation to make functional analysis the end of sociological inquiry—for then the discipline would be still-born. It is rather the end of sociology to explain— so-called "explained" functions: to show what things have a constant association with various functional or dysfunctional operations.

Nor can I accept the charge that this view of function and dysfunction prevents us from assigning any positive value to disturbance or growth. Stereotypic thinking sets the functional, dialectical, and evolutionary accounts of society in opposition. But they are not exclusive of one another, and the view I take gives a place to each. I see the process of social and cultural change as a two-phase or twin process, a kind of dialectic. There is first a disturbance where some positive state is lost. This may or may not be followed by a recovery of the same positive *state,* but that is not to say a restoration of the same *situation.* On the contrary, if recovery occurs, something new is added in order to achieve it, and this new thing added may be regarded as an evolutionary gain. There is a spiral. This is not unlike Toynbee's notion of growth through response to a challenge,[27] although I mean to be more scientific by naming the challenges and responses that groups experience perennially, whatever their scale. The evolutionary idea in it is close to Spencer's notion of increased differentiation and complexity.[28] But nothing more than this is claimed. It remains an open question whether people in groups that are "more advanced" in this sense are at all times better, happier, or richer because of it. The most that can be guaranteed is that their lives are more complicated and so have more potential. But I *am* claiming that there is a kind of "natural" inevitability about disturbance and that, if it is mastered there is growth; if it is not mastered there is deterioration. I should add that this does not imply an inevitable fluctuation, marked

26 D. Martindale, "Social Disorganization: The Conflict of Normative and Empirical Approaches," in *Modern Sociological Theory in Continuity and Change,* ed. H. Becker and A. Boskoff (New York: The Dryden Press, 1957), pp. 340–67.

27 A. J. Toynbee, *Civilization on Trial* (New York: Oxford University Press, 1948).

28 H. Spencer, *The Principles of Sociology* (New York: Appleton-Century-Crofts, 1882), Vol. I, 467–88.

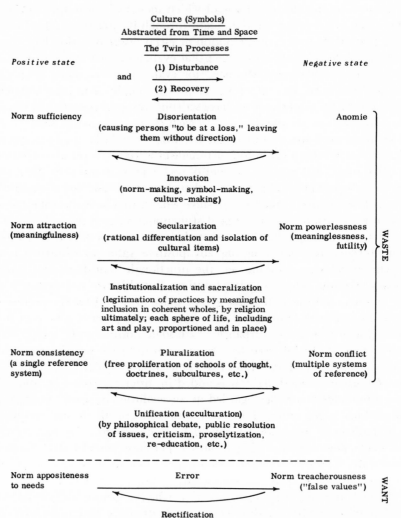

Figure I

Culture (Symbols)
Abstracted from Time and Space

The Twin Processes

Positive state   *Negative state*

(1) Disturbance
and
(2) Recovery

Norm sufficiency   Disorientation   Anomie
                        (causing persons "to be at a loss," leaving
                                them without direction)

Innovation
(norm-making, symbol-making,
culture-making)

Norm attraction   Secularization   Norm powerlessness
(meaningfulness)   (rational differentiation and isolation of   (meaninglessness,
                                    cultural items)   futility)

Institutionalization and sacralization
(legitimation of practices by meaningful
inclusion in coherent wholes, by religion
ultimately; each sphere of life, including
art and play, proportioned and in place)

Norm consistency   Pluralization   Norm conflict
(a single reference   (free proliferation of schools of thought,   (multiple systems
system)   doctrines, subcultures, etc.)   of reference)

Unification (acculturation)
(by philosophical debate, public resolution
of issues, criticism, proselytization,
re-education, etc.)

Norm appositeness   Error   Norm treacherousness
to needs   ("false values")

Rectification

WASTE

WANT

troughs of deterioration followed by crests of recovery. Although this
may occur, it is also possible that small increments of disturbance will be
followed by recovery almost instantaneously. When that occurs, the net
effect is a steady evolution.

We can, then, pin down four elements in a turn of the spiral: a positive state, a process of disturbance where there is movement from the
positive to a negative state, the negative state itself, and a process of recovery where there is movement in the opposite direction. A group's activity may pass from organization to disorganization and back; in the

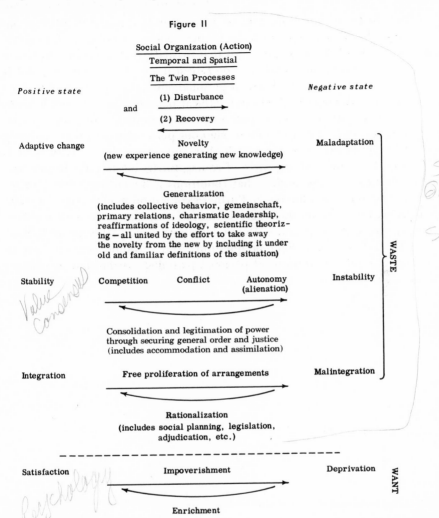

Figure II

same way, the condition of its culture may pass from what we must, for lack of terms, call *"culture"* to what we must, even more apologetically, call *"dysculture,"* and back. It is my purpose to name the component dimensions in this general social and cultural completeness or incompleteness. Figures I and II set them out in diagrammatic form. The two figures are matched. Component dimensions of the master concepts are represented as four levels, and each level in the one figure is the analogue of the corresponding position in the other. The fourth level, separated from the three above it in each diagram, refers more directly to the satisfaction of personal needs. The negative state on this level induces want, whereas the negative states above induce waste. By *waste,* I mean unrewarding effort. In these states, life goes on but action is directed to little or no effect: "the game is not worth the candle." Social pathology is *sui generis* and consists of the waste and want that twisted structures generate. Genuine sociological vision seems all too rare still, as I have lamented, and it is a pity so many think always of personal, clinical conditions when they think of pathology. But personal, clinical pathology is not even a necessary complication of social pathology. It is probable that most social pathology is generated by robust, vigorous personalities who are bursting with rude health: you can be all that and contribute to a life that is wasteful and unsatisfying. It is, of course, intriguing to ask whether, and to what extent, and under what conditions a life so lived may damage the mind (and even the body). Further exploration might reveal the main relationship to be mutual exacerbation, that is, that *given both together,* each makes the other worse. In any case, how social pathology itself arises and is relieved is a different question. And it would certainly not be correct to take indications of personal pathology as the sign or measure of social pathology.

chapter 7

The Dimensions of
Sociological Measurement:
I. The Components
of Culture

First in this chapter I must show the way in which I view culture. Unlike *social organization, culture* does not immediately convey the idea of a desideratum achieved, yet that is how I think it must be understood. *Social organization* does suggest something achieved and is helped by its negative, *social disorganization*. There does not seem to be a negative for *culture* that conveys the possibility of its being weak or being absent though wanted. *Anomie* is such a term for one aspect of culture, but there is no general negative. This "lack of a term" is itself illustrative of the lack it leaves undesignated. For culture has to be viewed as an assemblage of symbols whereby men represent their action in the world to themselves, and this stock of equipment may or may not be complete. Insofar as it is incomplete, individuals will be without guidance from the collectivity for their participation in the corporate life—they will be "at a loss," as we say. It is my purpose now to indicate the distinct ways in which this completeness is expressed and to suggest that each of them constitutes a dimension for measuring a property of cultures in general. Whenever we invoke these dimensions which we measure by evaluating, we evaluate by measuring.

I suggest that culture be viewed as consisting of symbols entirely. Malinowski pointed out that culture has two fundamental aspects: material culture, which is a body of artifacts, and a more inward, mental side, in which habits of thought and action invest the former with customary meanings.[1] The term *symbol* conveys the presence of both elements simul-

1 B. Malinowski, "Culture," *Encyclopaedia of the Social Sciences* (New York: The Macmillan Company, 1937).

taneously and that, after all, seems to be what Malinowski would wish. For symbols are recordings in material tokens of the meanings of social actions—although, in saying this, I mean *material* to include that in the constitution of man himself as well as that in his world. (My reason for adding this will soon be made plain.) Leslie A. White and George H. Mead have made us fully aware that meanings are things *between* people and that this externality necessarily involves a material symbolization.[2]

I must dissociate the use of *symbol* in what follows from one fairly common use of the term. This is a use that restricts the term to what is, after all, only a special class of cultural symbols, a class largely made up of expressive symbols: things like the flag, the cross, the wedding ring, the coat of arms, the uniform of office, the toast. True, these *are* symbols, but they represent only a part of the vast and varied range of symbols in culture. They belong with what I name higher-order symbols below. Each of them represents a muster of other symbols in order to indicate a sphere of common loyalty, and the particular action to which they summon us is a public affirmation of this loyalty. I mean something much more inclusive than this when I write of *symbols* here: I mean all signs generated by interaction to be means of communication by assuming meanings that are shared.

I understand the meaning of a symbol in the way Mead does: it is the whole state of subsequent involvement with one another that persons perceiving it acknowledge it to be summoning them to.[3] The meaning of a cultural symbol is some consummated cooperative act. Every word is a symbol, but so also are all customary gestures and actions presented with the aim of arresting the common attention and enlisting common cause. Every tool and manufactured article is a symbol, but so are all natural objects that are classified and named. We cannot escape the fact that the life of man is drenched with action, and social action at that, and that the meaning for him of anything whatsoever is what he anticipates will be the outcome of the whole social activity in which it is incorporated. We recognize this *kind* of situation existing readily enough in the case of words. Their meaning, we always allow, is decided by their context. It is the same with every kind of symbol.

But in what way is a customary action (like keeping to one side of the road) or a tool (like a screwdriver) or a natural object (like falling snow) analogous to a word and in fact a symbol? It is simply that, perceived to occur in a definite context by a group of persons, it is understood by them in common to be the cue for certain subsequent social actions. All these

---

[2] L. A. White, *The Science of Culture, A Study of Man and Civilization* (New York: Grove Press, Inc., 1949). G. H. Mead, *Mind, Self and Society from the Standpoint of a Social Behaviorist* (Chicago: The University of Chicago Press, 1959).

[3] *Ibid.*

things lodge in their experience as parts in a whole yet to be consummated and they are, by that fact, made symbols of meaning. Note what emerges about the connection between culture and personality once we acknowledge this: It is that all those customary actions we perform that are invested with conventional meanings and presented to a social audience *are culture.* It was to this I referred when I said the material in the constitution of man must be added to the other material at his disposal when taking inventory of his symbolic armory. This being the case, problems posed in terms of the relation between personality and culture can be self-defeating to a considerable degree: the two things are scarcely separable. Our actions are artifacts no less than our tools. Similarly, as we proceed to give them meanings and names by acting in the midst of them, the natural objects of our environment are artifacts. We even make what we innocently call our natural environment. So questions about the relation between culture and environment can likewise be pointless. It could be claimed that man does not live in nature at all, but makes his way through a forest of signaling symbols.

The great virtue in symbols is that by them man makes himself an "environment" that has generalized features. Cultural symbols are essentially abstractions: they shake loose a principle of good or worthwhileness from the particularities of time and place. Even so, quite commonly the prescription of an appropriate time and place for an action is written into them. But it is still a *typical* time and place, not a particular one: grace before meals, retiring before midnight, worship at church, football at the stadium, and so on. By making for himself these artificial time and space coordinates, man frees himself from determination by nature to a high degree. But he can achieve degrees of freedom beyond this. By knowing how part of an actual situation can symbolize the whole of it, he learns to invent arbitrary items to symbolize imaginary situations. Through symbols he can then envisage situations without actually entering them. You might say he has both first- and higher-order symbols. The latter symbolize thought-manipulations on symbols: the activity represented is mental. The door is a symbol inviting us to make exits and entrances. The word *door* is a symbol inviting us to conjure up ideal doors with ideal use possibilities, which of the uses we choose to consider being defined by the verbal context. In large measure, conversation is the cooperative mental activity for getting higher-order symbols in position to signal cooperative practical action.

I have already implied that meaning requires four things simultaneously; I must add a fifth. It includes first of all a forward orientation, an anticipation of consummation. It has to do secondly with cooperation, thirdly with consensus and, fourthly, it implies abstraction. But it also implies a need for commitment. For experiencing an action as part of a whole is only meaningful if the person endorses the whole as worthwhile. Another way of rendering the part-whole significance of symbols, then, might be as means-end significance. Symbols are meaningful when they are signals that authorize us to implement a means or end we believe in. They are norms or values. For the "wholes" to which our discrete actions are subordinated possess their unity by virtue of being sets of activities that culminate in some product we deem instrumentally or intrinsically good. Do we not make our "worlds," as we put it, around our different cardinal ends, rather in the way a pearl encrusts around a granule? This is how we come to build our basic institutions and to believe it fitting that our time and effort be portioned among them. We move from the world of the home to the world of politics to the world of religion to the world of leisure to the world of business—and so on. A coin has meaning because of the things it authorizes us to do in the world of business; strip that world away and a coin is a curiously molded bit of metal, if even that. The signaling power of symbols is of great importance: we make them ourselves, yet we set them beyond ourselves to have rule over us. We acknowledge authority in them and will take direction from them. We do so because, although they have no living voice, they have a *collective* one. This means that, although they may be inanimate, their power and life are actually mightier than those of the body: they are spiritual.

It is also of great importance that the worlds that give meanings to symbols are of increasing inclusiveness. Lesser worlds are swallowed up in greater ones—with a consequent deepening of meaning. A plate may symbolize the serving and eating of a course; the course is thus one of the first whole worlds, so to speak, of which the plate is a part. But the course belongs to the meal and in turn takes its meaning from that. And a single meal, however delectable, would be quite meaningless if it simply lodged in our experience by itself. A meal is meaningful as one of a succession of meals interspersed with fasting, as part of a whole pattern of nourishment for the sustaining of life. But, of course, it also enters into other worlds that intersect with the world of nourishment. Our meals are embellished to become part of the world of art. And insofar as we invite guests to share them with us, meals are expressive symbols of our solidarity with them. And so on. This is the kind of thing we mean when we say there are systems and subsystems in culture, analogous to those in social organization. Patterns are laid into more inclusive designs until we come at last to the whole meaning of life in the world. The idea of a pattern is a constantly recurring element in definitions of culture and also the idea that the pattern be for a whole way of life.[4] The meaning of *anything* for a man really derives from the meaning of *everything* for him. Proximate

[4] A. L. Kroeber and C. Kluckhohn, *Culture, A Critical Review of Concepts and Definitions* (New York: Vintage Books—Random House, Inc., 1963).

meaning flows back from ultimate meaning, not the other way around. Thus, although a man's perception of first and last things may be very dim and vague, and his perception of things confronting him vivid and distinct, the meaning for him of present things stems from his belief about first and last things. It is a condition of our existence we often find tantalizing that certainty and significance are inversely related. The pragmatic attitudes of the modern world leave man unfulfilled because they ignore this.

For nothing could be less in keeping with man's nature, really, than for him to become exclusively absorbed in the near at hand, to attack the most immediate or pressing problem first or dedicate his life to the service of his day and age. Man does not live by bread alone—but by meaning. Every culture shows us that the details of a people's everyday routine are meaningful and zestful insofar as their spiritual horizon is vast. Considerations of this kind must always be remembered when we represent man as a creature of needs. What does man need? Not discrete and varied gratifications, surely, but a meaningful harmony and ordering of gratifications and a subordination of each to the unity of all. In short, meaningfulness of life. It would be intellectually gauche, just as it could be morally pernicious, simply to say man needs sex, food, and play—to pick out just three. Man needs meaningful sex, meaningful food, and meaningful play. Ironically, when the meaning flies from his experience of these things he "needs" them more and more. Insatiability consumes him even as the possibility of satisfaction departs.

Man also needs dignity—which means a kind of self-awareness through adornment. It is not enough for him to have his adaptive needs met; he needs besides to know himself for a creature having those needs and to express that awareness. What he knows all too well is that his *need* is not satisfied if his *needs* are simply relieved, separately and one by one. His need will be satisfied to the degree his community achieves a cultural unity. All his art is an intimation of this unity that he craves. Not only the developed arts but decorative and ritual practices are fictional representations of it, like confessions of a faith that it will come. The fictional unity, the perfection, in every work of art and artistic flourish shows man communing with himself on his destiny. His need for leisure is a need for conditions under which he will come upon himself in this way. If he uses his spare time to improve his job potential or give community service, he will still need proper leisure beyond that. It is by having pleasures in leisure that man achieves the self-awareness he seeks. But artistic form must permeate all those pleasures that are apart from art as well as his art itself, if these are to be meaningful in turn. (What an intricacy of subtleties must be recognized to learn what man needs!) Man needs not simply relief for deficiency but pleasure—which is a kind of gratuity added. Yet his pleasures are a weary waste and distasteful unless they are made the medium of expressive symbolism. It is this that turns sensation into disinterested play. Pleasures must have form and design and thereby mirror in man's detachment the condition of success in his serious engagement: a cultural unity. Although Huizinga analyzes the expressions of play brilliantly,[5] he is inclined to leave the need for it unexplained as an ineffable mystery. He recognizes its connections with seriousness, but will not allow too close a relationship lest it detract from play's disinterestedness. I would suggest that, although disinterestedness is its essence, play arises from an imperative need of its own; namely, the need for dignity, and that it is a collaborator with seriousness in the ways I describe, rather than a thing wholly apart. Yet, again, the riches of art and play may entangle and leave man empty if they are given a sufficiency they do not have. For they are not his end but reminders of it to revive him in his struggle. On how fine a tightrope man walks to find satisfaction! Every good fails him if it is out of right order.

A culture is an ordering of symbols for a meaningful, dignified life.

Norm Sufficiency

The first level in Figure I (p. 86) deals purely with the *supply* of directions for living: are there enough, in view of our understanding of our situation? It is when these are not in adequate supply that disorientation ensues and we have the state of *anomie*, in Durkheim's sense.[6] There has been a tendency to make anomie a vast umbrella and to shove all cultural pathology under it. But this shows a lack of discrimination that constitutes a kind of intellectual anomie in itself. Anomie, essentially, is deficient discrimination, and I suggest there are at least three important cultural pathologies that are distinguishable from this. On the other hand, Merton gave currency to a restricted use of *anomie,* and there has been a certain tendency to make it mean only that.[7] An unequal emphasis on sanctioned goals and institutionalized means might possibly be considered one expression of anomie, but Durkheim was describing the more general condition of an absence of norms. A movement toward anomie, in Durkheim's sense, is the virtually inevitable beginning of one kind of social change. It only entails waste, however, if the positive response is not forthcoming. Although it has not been customary to connect *innovation* with *anomie,* Merton did this with his own meanings,[8] and I sug-

---

[5] J. Huizinga, *Homo Ludens, A Study of the Play-element in Culture* (Boston: Beacon Press, 1962), pp. 1–27.

[6] E. Durkheim, *Suicide, A Study in Sociology,* trans. J. A. Spaulding and G. Simpson, ed. with an introduction by G. Simpson (New York: The Free Press of Glencoe, Inc., 1951).

[7] R. K. Merton, *Social Theory and Social Structure* (New York: The Free Press of Glencoe, Inc., 1961), pp. 131–94.

[8] *Ibid.,* pp. 141–49.

gest that innovation, or one variety of it at least, is to be viewed as the
process of recovery from anomie. There has been ample discussion of
innovation in a general sense, but again we have to acknowledge a special
use of the term on Merton's part: He uses it to designate a case of deviant
behavior, for the innovation he refers to is a violation of existing norms.
But innovation in the usual sense of invention or the introduction of
inventions where they are still unknown—innovation with that meaning
is the filling of a cultural void and can scarcely be considered deviance
at all. Indeed, because deviance must have a norm to violate, even to
speak of deviance where there is anomie seems contradictory. Innovations,
in whatever department of life they appear, are all new symbols to guide
our course more exactly. Furthermore, they all represent new meetings
of the mind, new agreements. Although we tend to emphasize the loneli-
ness of the inventor—and it is surely real enough—an invention is only
implanted in a culture through the endorsement of its adopters.

Norm Attraction (Meaningfulness)

The second level of Figure I deals with the *aggregation* of the directions for living: Do they cohere? This involves a principle like gravity or
mass in culture. The discrete particles, the normative symbols for particular actions and situations, have to be bundled or lumped together in
wholes. Once a whole is formed it attracts to itself, by a kind of gravity,
new and isolated items. I have already enlarged on this pursuit of meaning in the social process and need add little concerning its general nature.
It is well recognized if only by implication, and there are writers on social
pathology who have placed their emphasis on a deficiency in this condition rather than on anomie. They describe a situation in which norms
are present and plainly symbolized, but fail to compel. Broadly speaking,
this is the definition ascribed to social disorganization by Faris in his book
by that title, and by Elliott and Merrill in their book by the same title.[9]
It is because life is fragmented that disenchantment spreads throughout
all of it. The individual finds himself in a maze of blind alleys, his good
intentions become *non sequiturs,* ridiculous postures are forced on him
by his conscientiousness. It is Kafka's world, where frustration is king.
Very close to this was the conception of social disorganization used by
Thomas and Znaniecki in *The Polish Peasant,* although their stress was
on a specific factor in the situation.[10] They saw the segmentation of life
in complex societies producing a moral overloading: because there is
no adjudicator or regulator among the departments of life to indicate

[9] R. E. L. Faris, *Social Disorganization* (New York: The Ronald Press Company,
1955). M. A. Elliott and F. E. Merrill, *Social Disorganization* (New York: Harper &
Row, Publishers, Inc., 1961).

[10] W. I. Thomas and F. Znaniecki, *The Polish Peasant in Europe and America*
(New York: Alfred A. Knopf, Inc., 1927), pp. 1831–914.

how big a claim each department might make on us, the best of us can no more than partially fulfil his duties. Ogburn's notion of a cultural lag belongs here as well: [11] the idea that change in one department of life necessitates changes in other departments and that the latter may be slow in coming. We then sense that the different sides of our life are out of step with each other.

The single overall concept which expresses this fracturing of life's unity is *secularization*—as Redfield and Becker used the term.[12] It comes essentially from the invasion of our living arrangements by greater reason, for the sake of greater efficiency. Whether the closed mind is forced open by outside contact or by direct reflection, it becomes free to compare what is with what might be "better" in this sense. There is a more gratuitous kind of innovation at work here. But our aim is to substitute one means for an existing one rather than to fill a void, which is the case with the innovating response to anomie. What distinguishes secularization is a repudiation of tradition in order to tear reviewable practices out of context. Separate sides of life receive separate—and very likely unequal—attention. The result is a proliferation of disconnected specialisms that leaves men searching for the unity in their total life. Although we are inclined to celebrate the emancipating effects of secularization, we often forget that the splintering, shallowness, and sensed futility of which we complain in the same situation are traceable to the same source.

For secularization only yields a net gain if there is recovery. There has to be institutionalization of the improved practices and, ultimately, sacralization once more. It has not been customary to view sacralization as the full flowering of the process of institutionalization, yet this is how it should, I believe, be regarded. Institutionalization is essentially a two-sided process of keeping up a valued practice and building it into a whole. The practice is cut down to size even as steps are taken to perpetuate it, and it is thus legitimated. The religious quest is simply this same operation in its most inclusive reach. A people's postulation of a supernatural is an action of exactly the same kind as their pursuit of a political union or an integrated family. The supernatural they postulate is simply the wholeness in their total involvement with life, just as government is the wholeness in their political life and family unity the wholeness in their domestic life. The whole is always more than the sum of its parts and where it is the wholeness of the totality of things that is concerned, the "something more" is experienced and described as *super*natural. That men repeatedly push through to the supernatural in their pursuit of

[11] W. F. Ogburn, *Social Change with Respect to Culture and Original Nature* (Gloucester, Mass.: Peter Smith, 1950).

[12] R. Redfield, *The Folk Culture of Yucatan* (Chicago: The University of Chicago Press, 1941). H. Becker, *Through Values to Social Interpretation, Essays on Social Contexts, Actions, Types, and Prospects* (Durham, N.C.: Duke University Press, 1950).

meaning, and take it for their only guarantor of meaning, is simply a fact for sociology to receive. Some of the most sensitive nerves in the social organism can only be dissected when religion is accepted in this capacity. It is a pity so few moderns can take the relaxed attitude to religion that would let them accord it its proper character as a social fact. No doubt every religion has a theology, but not all questions concerning the nature of religion are theological. What *face* men may rightfully give to the supernatural is a theological question. What *place* they give to the pursuit of it and how and why they engage it are sociological questions. If there be any who do not concern themselves with the supernatural explicitly yet devote their lives to values, it comes to the same thing so far as "wholeing" is concerned. For values are ends men seek for their own sake, and anything set above the mundane in that way envelops it in a unitary meaning. Dogma or no, there is a beginning of religion in values. Conversely, the worship of holiness is not strictly distinguishable from the passion for wholeness in value commitment.

Norm Consistency

The third level in Figure I might not appear to be distinct from the second, yet it refers to different matters. It portrays the situation in which cultural closure has proceeded to a degree, but more than one way of attempting it has evolved. The problem men experience here is what is most commonly called *culture conflict.* Their problem is not that they know of *no* order that will give meaning and conviction to their lives, but that they are aware that competing orders are claiming allegiance from them. The conflict may be between the culture of a person's group and that of another group, but if he has identified with both groups he will have taken the conflict into himself and become a marginal man. Ethnic relations have been analyzed in these terms, as well as interclass and interfaith relations. The cultural frontier around the world between Western man and former colonials is shaken now with the efforts to cast this sickness off.

Whether within a man or between men who must make one life together, this situation breeds its own kind of waste. Whereas anomie bespeaks a lack of direction and the harvest of secularization is a lack of conviction, culture conflict spells a lack of decision or accord. Durkheim's account of anomie was very largely in terms of the insatiability an individual experiences when his desires are not limited by social norms. He considered that norms are necessary to channel desire into purposive action. More recently, the inward experience accompanying the outward lack of norms has been called *anomia,* and attempts have been made to factorize it. Surprisingly, we do not find prominence given to insatiability in this, and the array of factors is miscellaneous and unsystematic. Srole has even assimilated the notion of *alienation* to anomie,[13] but this seems to have little to do with the case—at least in any sociological meaning of that versatile term. For *social* alienation is essentially a withdrawal of identification from a still viable system of norms: there has to be a defined system to be alienated from. Not surprisingly, work like Srole's has inspired little following and has provoked criticism.[14] Until we have a sharper conceptualization in this whole area, I prefer to think simply and to discriminate in the above manner between the inner states that accompany the different cultural pathologies.

Park and Stonequist have made the *marginal man* famous.[15] Cohen has pointed to *unintegrated subcultures,* Brown to *unintegrated ideologies,* Bernard to *"value inconsistency,"* by which she referred to a condition that others have recognized—a discrepancy between what people say they want and what they really want.[16] It might be better called *cultural duplicity,* for there is a subterranean or *sub rosa* life sanctioned that makes hypocrisy out of much public conduct. Yinger identified the emergent subculture that actively resists another culture and called this *contra-culture.*[17] Cultural pluralism exists in other expressions. The *ism* that turns *psychology* into *psychologism, science* into *scientism,* and so on, denotes the tendency to create a cultural closure around some restricted, arbitrary point of view. It courts inevitable conflict with other *isms,* of course. Snow's divergent *"cultures"* belong with these.[18]

Cultural pluralism is intolerable to man, and the fact that many moderns live in this condition in the family and with neighbors and work-associates must account for a great deal of anxiety, although it has many other handicaps besides. We make much of the virtue of tolerance, but tolerance is only a virtue if it is a temporary truce to compose differences. We have to share one culture in the end or live to a considerable degree to no effect. We also extol the virtues of the pluralist society as a condi-

13 L. Srole, "Social Integration and Certain Corollaries: An Exploratory Study," *American Sociological Review,* 21 (1956), 709–16.

14 See M. B. Clinard, ed., *Anomie and Deviant Behaviour: A Discussion and Critique* (London: The Free Press of Glencoe, 1964), and H. McLosky and J. J. Schaar, "Psychological Dimensions of Anomy," *American Sociological Review,* 30 (1965), 14–40.

15 R. E. Park, "Human Migration and the Marginal Man," *American Journal of Sociology,* 33 (1928), 881–93. E. V. Stonequist, *The Marginal Man: A Study in Personality and Culture Conflict* (New York: Russell & Russell, 1961).

16 A. K. Cohen, *Delinquent Boys, The Culture of the Gang* (New York: The Free Press of Glencoe, Inc., 1960). L. G. Brown, *Social Pathology, Personal and Social Disorganization* (New York: Appleton-Century-Crofts, 1942). J. Bernard, *American Community Behavior* (New York: Holt, Rinehart & Winston, Inc., 1965).

17 J. Yinger, "Contraculture and Subculture," *American Sociological Review,* 25 (1960), 625–35.

18 C. P. Snow, *The Two Cultures and the Scientific Revolution* (New York: Cambridge University Press, 1959).

tion of democracy, following Montesquieu and Tocqueville.[19] Yet this refers to a plurality of centers of force under the *one* culture, so that power checks power. It would be a flagrant misrepresentation of this view to think that these classical authors would advocate *cultural* pluralism as having virtue. On the contrary, Tocqueville took for the key condition of liberty in America the sectarian religion the New Englanders held in common, an approach the Roman Catholics among them shared.[20] It was, he thought, so agreeably suited to their political independence from one another while producing the moral discipline without which that independence would merely drag them apart. One final defense seems to be wrung from anyone who insists on the functionality of cultural unity. Whenever this is advocated, so many modern minds fly to visions of monolithic, totalitarian states. But one can only say there are more ways to unity than by the violent, political suppression of differences and, as for that, the occurrence of totalitarianism itself suggests that there are limits to the diversity a people can endure.[21] Cultural pluralism can be enriching, but only if it is resolved in a subsequent unification. Park had no wish to arrest the emergence of marginal men, for instance; [22] their agony is the crucible of another civilization if it succeeds in unifying their mixed allegiances. The unification process may possibly select common elements from the competing cultures as well as the more universal elements from each, while sanctioning as options practices that are not directly opposed. Unless there is to be prodigious waste, there can only be one culture for one nation and ultimately, we may presume, one culture for one world.

Norm Appositeness to Needs

The misapplication or right application of effort that has been considered so far has to do with the orderliness of relations between the elements of culture; that is to say, between symbols. But the key symbols themselves may be for or against us depending on whether they give directions apposite to our needs. The key symbols are the ones that define our self-sufficient ends, our values; and these are infinitely vulnerable, subject to a malady that may strike us at the quick. It is possible for a culture to be free from the defects we have considered so far, yet infected with this other sickness. To exchange the metaphor for an ancient one, it is possible for the structure of the cultural house to be faultless and

---

[19] Baron de Montesquieu, *The Spirit of the Laws* (New York: Hafner Publishing Co., Inc., 1949). Alexis de Tocqueville, trans. Henry Reeve, rev. Francis Bowen, ed. Phillips Bradley, *Democracy in America* (New York: Alfred A. Knopf, Inc., 1945).

[20] *Ibid.*, Vol. II, 20–30.

[21] Cf. E. Fromm, *Escape from Freedom* (New York: Holt, Rinehart & Winston, Inc., 1960).

[22] Park, *op. cit.*

for the house to be built on sand. I refer to the state of affairs against which the prophets speak, where men spend their money for that which is not bread and their labor for that which satisfieth not. Commonly we call it the worship of idols or the pursuit of false values. This is a legitimate dimension of sociological measurement, too. It is mainly the social critics who have made it their target of attack, and these writers have not always been intellectually disciplined. But there are more rigorous sociologists who make this pathology their study. Two books that sustain this point of view in accounting for the state of society are Bredemeier and Toby's *Social Problems in America* and Henry's *Culture Against Man.*[23]

One does not have to dwell on the proneness of humans to fall into error. It seems we are forever blind and, like the character in Tolstoy's tale,[24] do not know our own needs. The way to recovery does exist. But it takes the hero's sacrifice of speaking out and being reviled. The prophets rebuke our folly and are inevitably stoned. It is the measure of their magnanimity that they are willing to take the punishment, confident of vindication to come. On the day that we vindicate them we have sided with them, so by their stripes we are healed. Then in the unity of their following they have a resurrection life that is not confined like their former life. Error, by itself, is an unqualified deterioration and spells only loss. But if it is countered by the costly rectification it needs, there is only gain. The evolution confronting us here, apparently, is the mystery of redemption.

We may pause on the saddle of this and the succeeding chapter to weigh some of the implications of the argument. I have been insisting that it is the task of sociology to identify the states and measure the transforming processes that characterize a group at any time, and to look for constant relationships between these properties. It seems that dedication to this undertaking would **not** only unify the discipline but would resolve old issues within it.

When sociology is allowed this exclusively intellectual competence it is divorced from every particular commitment to action, yet it remains available for application to every cause, even opposed causes. Knowledge is then clearly seen in its true light. It is a thing like money, fluid wealth that can strengthen any cause, be the cause good or evil. Yet this science is not trivial or cold in relation to humanity, as some seem to think a

23 H. C. Bredemeier and J. Toby, *Social Problems in America, Costs and Casualties in an Acquisitive Society* (New York: John Wiley & Sons, Inc., 1961). J. Henry, *Culture Against Man* (New York: Random House, Inc., 1963).

24 L. N. Tolstoy, "What Men Live By," in *Two Tales,* trans. R. T. Currall (London: George G. Harrap & Company, Ltd., n.d.).

science of conduct must be. The questions it asks are the very ones that are of burning concern to living, suffering people. Their "social problems" are its intellectual concern, so much its concern that it is pointless to make a separate field of study out of "social problems" or to suggest that interest in them makes anyone a "special" kind of sociologist. The ideologies of people are its concern also, and so much so that it is pointless to make a special study of the sociology of knowledge. Indeed, "the sociology of knowledge" has begun to consist of the historical sociologists discovering what the anthropological sociologists already knew as *culture.*

It will be obvious that throughout my analysis I have been skating close to every kind of thing on which men wax passionate, controversial, and even violent: I am trespassing on ideologies. For it is in their ideologies that men make their own diagnosis of the condition of their cultures and pledge to uphold or amend them. Yet by preserving a characterizing treatment myself and avoiding an appraising one, it has been possible for me to stop short of advocating any ideology of my own. Once we believe it is possible to do this, a tremendous new space opens to our life. It means that we can accept proposals for reform and political and religious dogmas for what they are—irreplaceable ingredients of our life—but also that we are to some extent equipped to judge them. This can be especially useful when we have to judge between opposing ones. Insofar as the science of sociology makes progress and its findings diffuse into popular culture, remedies proposed for social problems as well as ideologies advanced will be asked to defend themselves on objective grounds. And the way will exist for them to undertake this defense.

chapter 8

The Dimensions of
Sociological Measurement:
II. The Components
of Social Organization

Culture, I have tried to suggest, is a fluid currency, a store or bank of symbolic equipment, that man lays up for use as he may require. Man has been called "culture bound," but it is only as a willing slave he need be so. For at any given instant he is free to decide whether and which cultural directives apply to his situation. The discontinuity between culture and social organization is the razor edge of the present moment. Certainly, for most routines we are glad to have the machine of culture rule us and thereby save us thought, for there are limits to the innovation we can implement at one time. Yet, even so, we continually exercise *options* among the available cultural directives that *could* be applied to the place where we stand. For instance, we usually let the day of the week and the time of day automatically dictate what we do. But from time to time we have no compunction in setting the standard routine aside—for the special occasion or unusual circumstance. What we do then will almost certainly be something else that is culturally prescribed; but what materializes in practice, in social organization, is a consequence of choice. It is not stretching things to say that choice is operating too when we simply consent to follow routine. Herein lies much of the importance of distinguishing between culture and social organization. Social organization is what materializes in practice on particular occasions when culture is filtered through choice. The more alert the people acting, the more willing and discriminating those choices can be.

Like many other distinctions that have to be drawn in sociology, that between culture and social organization has to be drawn with great delicacy. For one thing, we must not suppose that, because they are distinct, one can have no representation in the other. A cultural standard is always incarnated in any organizational act, so culture spreads its charge through all man's deeds. At all particular times and places it makes its appearance, yet this is not incompatible with the definition that, as culture, it is abstracted from time and place. There is the further point that organization may materialize once for all or be repeated. A morning tea party that meets only once will assume an organizational form: if the decision is taken to keep meeting every Tuesday, a fairly standard pattern of organization will probably result. What is the group's organization? What it does at any one time, or what it repeats every time? Is what it repeats on successive occasions perhaps its culture? It seems these questions must be answered in the following way: Activity, even if it is successively repeated, constitutes organization. The organization of a group that meets but once is the arrangement once enacted. A group whose life is realized through reassembly has its organization described at two levels: the standard or typical organization that recurs as it reassembles, and the variations or embellishments peculiar to each separate occasion. According to the purpose we have in mind, we will describe one or both levels when we give an account of a group's organization. As for the repetitive element being equated with culture—strictly speaking, only the *symbolized standards* that are consciously held in view as repetitively applicable constitute culture.

It is for the purpose of allowing the same elements of social organization to unfold time and again that culture is made, of course. A number of studies have been published under the rubric "Culture and Personality." Yet the relation between culture and social organization is the sociological question par excellence, and has not been explored as much as one would expect. It is by now a truism, for instance, that the cultures of different peoples vary; this is generally thought to present a practical obstacle to the harmony of mankind. Yet the diversity of cultures is rarely traced into the diversity of social organization that the peoples of the world have evolved in different situations. The relevance, to immigrant groups, of their original culture has to be tested by the same considerations. Is there not a time, after a transitional phase, when much of it becomes baggage to be shed? Again, it is sometimes glibly stated that "whereas culture shapes individuals, individuals shape culture." There is scarcely any truth in this. Individuals alone do not hammer on culture to change it: it is the shifts in the organization of relations between individuals that new cultural symbols record, and these shifts are effected through interaction. Social organization has to be considered apart from culture because it tends to be fluid where culture is fixed. It is the arena where life tests what thought commends. At the same time, of course, culture has its own fluidity in comparison with which organization appears fixed. For thought can range free from action and visualize new forms for it that can be given symbolic representation. Culture and social organization are in a game of tag; each has its own freedom to lead the chase where it will.

But to what, precisely, do we refer when we speak of *social organization?* Essentially, I think, it is to the stabilization of rational practices. The terms *social cohesion* and *solidarity* should be considered virtually synonymous with it. Sociometry attenuated the meaning of *cohesion* to an affectional tie between persons.[1] Yet this makes a wan substitute for Durkheim's important concept of *social solidarity.*[2] Durkheim recognized two principles of solidarity: mutual dependence (*organic solidarity*) and a common conscience (*mechanical solidarity*). Here we have the co-activity in roles and the shared expectation concerning it to which reference was made in Chapter 5. Durkheim began by taking these for alternative sources of solidarity. Yet in the end he seemed to think that they are not mutual substitutes and that neither could suffice alone. I myself find it hard to consider them alternatives. Is it not their *coincidence* that binds people together? In the mutual dependence of tasks rationality is effected, in the shared expectation stability secured. This rationality requirement presents both an external and an internal challenge to social organization, the stability requirement an internal challenge.

Adaptive Change

The external challenge to social organization is to cope with "present and foreseeable circumstances." This is the requirement represented in the first level of Figure II (p. 87). Change in its external situation may force a group to "make rearrangements," but a change in its knowledge of the same situation can have the same effect. (A changed view of the justice of existing arrangements is but an instance of the latter.) The ultimate source of the external impulse to change, therefore, is new knowledge—or probably more correct still, novel experience. Washburne has proposed the overwhelming event as the source of all social change, and thereby simplifies our thinking about it considerably.[3] But there seems no reason why an event should be of overwhelming proportions in order to force social change, so long as it is of overwhelming novelty.

[1] H. H. Jennings, *Leadership and Isolation, A Study of Personality in Inter-Personal Relations,* 2nd ed. (New York: Longmans, Green & Co., Inc., 1950); J. L. Moreno, *Who Shall Survive? Foundations of Sociometry, Group Psychotherapy and Sociodrama* (Beacon, N.Y.: Beacon House, Inc., 1953); J. L. Moreno, et al., eds., *The Sociometry Reader* (New York: The Free Press of Glencoe, Inc., 1960).

[2] E. Durkheim, *The Division of Labor in Society,* trans. G. Simpson (New York: The Free Press of Glencoe, Inc., 1960).

[3] N. F. Washburne, *Interpreting Social Change in America* (New York: Random House, Inc., 1954).

Man's intelligence and sensibility impose on him a growing burden of new knowledge; to accommodate, he must change his ways continually. He has no option but to be put at a loss through having one day's practice made unequal to the next day's knowledge.

He does have some option, though, in his reaction to this. This is essentially man's confrontation in life with anomie in his culture: procedures and norms for dealing with perceived realities are lacking. Individuals can be torpedoed by this experience or seek recovery; that is, both a negative and positive reaction are possible. One instance of the negative, maladaptive reaction is the anomic suicide that Durkheim identified.[4] Other instances, that do not require departing from life altogether, are the various forms of pseudoconformity commonly styled "hypocrisy." Such are the "bohemian" and "philistine" stances described by Thomas and Znaniecki [5]—are the "other-directedness" and "tradition-directedness" of Riesman [6] identical with them? Knowing that standard practice has been made irrelevant by wider experience, but not knowing what to put in its place, the person involves himself either with a foreground scene-shifting effort or with the immutable past. In either case his life is a time-biding front.

But the positive, adaptive reaction, whereby recovery is achieved, is one of reorganization. On the cultural level this demands innovation. But on the level of action, what is it we see people doing to achieve this state? Not infrequently there is a denouement of collective behavior and ideology. By collective behavior in some form men make a primitive communication of sharing in a predicament, and then, in resurgent ideology they reaffirm their responsibility to one another *as whole men.* Ideologies characteristically reckon with two matters: they propose a remedy for the immediate breakdown, but they also remind men that their lasting obligation to one another is more diffuse than that prescribed by the collapsing structure. They are "brothers," "comrades," "human beings." This tides them over the breakdown in their specialized role obligations and prepares them for a different definition of duties. The same rallying force inherent in collective behavior and ideology resides in charismatic leadership. What is it that is so perennially appealing in this? It is simply that it reconstitutes order at a high level of generality. Someone, someone more dependent on order than his fellows perhaps, is able to reinfuse it into the collective activity. He is able to successfully insist on the importance of a plan, a program, a pattern of living, a world view. The novelty that dis-

4 E. Durkheim, *Suicide, A Study in Sociology,* trans. J. A. Spaulding and G. Simpson, ed. G. Simpson (London: Routledge & Kegan Paul, Ltd., 1952).

5 W. I. Thomas and F. Znaniecki, *The Polish Peasant in Europe and America* (New York: Dover Publications, Inc., 1958).

6 D. Riesman, in collaboration with R. Denney and N. Glazer, *The Lonely Crowd* (New Haven: Yale University Press, 1950).

concerted his fellows has left him still resourceful. There remains a universal condition of successful action in order, to which he clings. He is more attached to this principle apparently than to the institutions, now shaken, that hitherto gave expression to it.

In an earlier chapter, I suggested that cooperation in struggle is the concept of *community* having the most potential for sociology. At this point, *community* with that meaning finds its place in my argument. For this, too, is part of man's resource in maladaptation. Another point made earlier is that it is not enough for man to have his adaptive needs met— he needs to ornament his life as well. The community bond seems to have its roots in a marriage of these needs. They *are* wedded in some inscrutable way, for the outcry men always make in crisis is not simply that their survival is threatened but their civilization. They then close ranks. Community might be viewed as the pressure their closeness generates to lift men, first to survival certainly, but quite beyond survival into civilization.

For we may think of civilization as the dignifying of human existence through adornment, achieved by the exploitation of surplus to devise need-gratifications not strictly related to survival. In urban-industrial society, luxury resources for this purpose reach vast quantities; but some resources may be diverted to it by man at any level of culture. Civilization thus conceptualized necessarily imposes a problem of maintaining productive cooperation. Mutual trust must be maintained throughout the society in the face of numbers and specialization. Increase in membership and specialization is what allows an elaboration of production, but it can only be guaranteed if mutual trust persists. When that is present, identification occurs. Then the curbs put on inclination for the sake of social organization are not irksome. The aggression born of frustration is directed against the obstacles to order, and is not destructive.

It is to keep this fount of trust open in the midst of the garden of civilization that men foster community among themselves. For this is the society within society, the pitch of mutuality, not assured by nature, to which they have continually to stir one another up. Like Heaven, community is not a place, and whether it exists among the people of a place is a matter for inspection. It is essentially a matter of their keeping their likeness in evidence, so that the solidarity from sympathy will counter the centrifugal forces of differentiation and scale. The most elementary likeness is kinship, and the rudimentary community is the kin group. When community has extended beyond this, it is because men were prepared to extend the kinship prerogatives to persons involved in one struggle with them. The struggle against the natural habitat, and the struggles for the viability of race, class, and faith, seem to be the main ones which have served. The one struggle leaves the one mark, and with it comes the consciousness of kind.

People baptized into "brotherhood" by any of these affinities have sought to sponsor a common life among themselves through basic institutions, and among themselves exclusively so far as possible. Aware, however, that life's emergencies are never wholly provided for through these, they have acknowledged reserve obligation to one another as well: over and above their laid-down duties they pledge mutual help in ways that do not have to be specified in advance. They entrust the ordering of their affairs to a community authority to which they give their full devotion. And they become jealous guardians of their unique culture, especially of those supererogatory artifacts which constitute their adornment and dignity. If men bring out their likenesses to generate community, it is so they will be prepared, by all these resources, for the challenges that will come.

I am aware that a seemingly contrary notion exists, wherein civilization is thought to be a product of cosmopolitanism rather than community, and is thought to flower under civil government which confers citizenship on a diversity of men, even some former aliens (a view that Diamond examines [7]). Yet this is simply the case of the extension of kinship prerogatives to those who are prepared to align themselves with a territorial struggle. Naturally, there will be hybrid vigor in the cultural mixture that will make the civilization richer. But to confer citizenship on a man is to recognize him as a fellow in the political cause. Actually, it seems quite a mistake to set the civic and communal principles in opposition to one another. The truth concerning their apparent difference is rather this: the civic allegiance of the citizen expresses a particularly sophisticated development of the communal tie we recognize much more readily in rudimentary forms like kinship and race. There is, of course, a sense in which citizenship makes the person's distinctiveness the ground of his likeness: there is a heady admixture in it of the organic and mechanical principles of solidarity. By being yoked with the role of citizen, one's special capacities are made tributary to the common good. He is acknowledged to be the *same* as others by virtue of the fact that they each make *different* contributions to a commonwealth.

The *burden* of a civilization, incidentally, as distinct from the problem of its source, is to put its ornaments to an innocent use. For a society has to devise ornamental gratifications which are indeed satisfying, each of which takes its place in relation to the others, and which together are not subversive of survival needs. The possibility is that men will lose dignity, and even adaptability, through the things whose creation confers

7 S. Diamond, ed., *Primitive Views of the World* (New York and London: Columbia University Press, 1964), pp. v–xxix, 170–93.

the possibility of dignity on them. They can become enslaved by an inordinate or inappropriate attachment to their ornaments. Presumably this is one of the universal principles enshrined in the idea of fetishism. Man becomes dependent on things which he has himself gratuitously made meaningful, and is degraded by his own trifles. This is what we mean by "vice," and it is a universal possibility. How far their civilization adds dignifying virtue to men and how far it entangles them in vice is one of the perennial sociological questions.

As well as large-scale changes, changes have constantly to be made within the minutiae of life. Even in those safe places of society where norms are firmly established, the norms rarely fit the case exactly. It is therefore required that the actors themselves supply an informal, on-the-spot structure like an inner lining to the formal. Both for these minor adaptations and for major ones, the recruits to any social system need to come equipped in advance to do both more and different things than the rules prescribe. Here is a critical instance of the past laying its hand on the present. For what reasserts itself here is nurture, not biological nature. It is the *human* nature which is fashioned in the primary group that constitutes this regenerative capacity, and if any man has been denied this group he will be denied this nature and capacity also. If ideology is man's theory of recovery, the imprint of his primary group involvements is his empirical basis for the theory. In the primary group, men will have experienced the unrestricted mutuality, the universal love, which acts like embryonic tissue for the secondary structures that can grow anew between them wherever their ways drift into chaos.

Why has it seemed appropriate to link collective behavior, ideology, charismatic leadership, community, and primary group? It is simply that they are all expressions of the elasticity in groups that enables them to accommodate novelties and adapt. They are united by their ability to take away the novelty from the new by including it under old, familiar definitions of the situation. (Scientific theorizing and all generalizing thought are allied with them.) They point ahead by pointing back, for they primitivize experience exactly at the point where experience is making unprecedented demands. The operation is essentially a process that Smelser has delineated with great insight, although Blumer had also made reference to it.[8] This is why I have chosen to use Smelser's term *generalization* to group this range of phenomena together—although Smelser only used it with reference to the beliefs that guide collective behavior. What happens in all cases is that experience, as men share it, is lived on a more general level for a time. They peel back their masks to that level where

8 N. J. Smelser, *Theory of Collective Behavior* (New York: The Free Press of Glencoe, Inc., 1962), pp. 79–130. H. Blumer, "Collective Behavior," in *Principles of Sociology*, 2nd ed., ed. A. M. Lee (New York: Barnes & Noble, Inc., 1957), pp. 199–200.

their relationship to each other is more diffuse and less differentiated, more schematic, as if giving attention to this familiarity made the strangeness in their situation easier to bear. Their mutuality is intensified, as though the pleasure received from it made the pain of rational change the more tolerable.

For we have not lost sight of the fact that it is a growing load of rationality that is being cushioned by all this. (I mean practical rationality, of course, in the sense of activities articulated to effect ends. How much deliberate thought this involves, and on the part of how many, is another matter.) What has to be done in life to give effect to new knowledge is to alter the division of labor. New equipment and roles will perhaps crowd in, old roles be differently defined. The "generalization" that occurs to make that possible is like a melting of social materials into their most fluid state so that they will be optimally available for reshaping.

The resiliency or adaptability we look for in social systems when making functional analysis requires them to meet novelties by absorbing them in these ways, rather than be shattered by shock. It shows misunderstanding when critics of functionalism represent it as opposed to change. It is not opposed to change in social systems, but it registers a sense of loss if costly structures collapse when they still have work to do. If some novelty should leave men unable to cope completely, that would not be social change, but social extinction. It is from knowing that human life is impossible without society and society impossible without adaptive change that the functionalist marks down this bleak alternative. Yet attempts to defend the usefulness of functional analysis for the study of change have not exploited the fact that an adaptation requirement means that a readiness to change must be maintained. Far from opposing change, functionalism expects it.

Stability

Now let us consider the internal challenge to social organization of the stability requirement. It is shown as the second level of Figure II. This is a challenge to motivate lasting support. Stability is secured in social arrangements only if everyone involved in them is "satisfied with them"—at the very least "prepared to put up with them." Everyone must have his reward or the guarantee of it. Thus the maintenance of stability is essentially a matter of the enlistment of motives. (Lest, on the mention of this, thoughts turn to the psychology of motivation, I must insist *that* is not our problem. *Enlistment* is the operative word, and the sociological question concerns the *distribution* of rewards and their *conferral by social agents*.) Although every person's reward will not be the same, everyone will have been given the same expectation of a certain reward and hence share a positive regard for, or valuation of, the arrangements. If we say, without further qualification, that value-consensus is the basis of social order, we probably claim too much if we mean more than this. But where this is lacking in even a single individual there will be disorganization in some degree, however localized. The individual's guarantee of reward is his security, and conformity to the arrangements of the group is what he will give in return. In this lies the group's power of control over him, and the insurance of its own organization at the same time. A consensus of this kind, and security for and control of individuals, are therefore further indices of social normality.

And yet the question of a consensus in values is not to be disposed of so summarily. While it may not be necessary that people hold the same ultimate values for them to cooperate for specific purposes, it does seem likely that people who are willing to take responsibility for maintaining a total community will be sharers of the same values. Mutual support in the procurement of values is the only reward commensurate with that weighty burden. Thus under the protection, as it were, of the leaders' overarching harmony, a multitude of more contractual, exploitive, and parasitic relationships can breed: the exchange relationship of commerce is perhaps the commonest. For the sake of the specific and expedient reward, there will be many men willing to hold their values out of view. They will keep their thoughts to themselves in order to live off the elite of the community in general. Although the order of any total community could rest on a consensus in values between some, there could be any number of pockets within it whose order would simply require a consensus of a much more limited kind, viz., a shared regard for the arrangements whereby everyone is to have his reward—what we ordinarily call "an agreement," or "an understanding." We might also note that communication of a certain effectiveness will be necessary if everyone involved is to know what these arrangements are and if consensus is to be reached in upholding them.

But we can say more. Whether individuals are satisfied with their rewards depends largely on whether they think them fair in comparison with the rewards of others. Any social system at all is in danger of being convulsed if a supposed injustice is unearthed—although the convulsion does not necessarily occur. The victim may grin and bear it if he thinks rebellion will prove more costly of justice still. Or there may be sanctioned channels through which he will work for a change. But, on the other hand, he may harbor resentment and be uncooperative, or take the law into his own hands and fight for his rights.

Insofar as rewards are left without assignment to named parties, men may be driven into competition for them. There is no reason to think this is all negative in its effects. It is a good device for the awakening of motivation and, insofar as the relative suitability of different candidates is not known, a good device for selection. It can introduce instability of certain kinds, however. To the extent that no one knows what to expect regarding the outcome, competition rocks the boat. To the extent that no one sees reason for it, there can be resentment against the authorities that did not protect everyone's entitlement and left things so much to chance. It can also be wasteful if potential cooperators are made competitors in such a way that their net gain operating separately is less than the gain would have been had they worked together. (Leaving aside the question of whether and at what point the tendency should be resisted, this evident wastefulness in much competition would explain the tendency for perfect competition to shift in the direction of partnership and monopoly.) Competition can also be wasteful in that competitors, instead of qualifying for different, complementary roles, strive to qualify for the same role. Perhaps only the winners will continue in the role. In this case, the others will have to learn to be satisfied with something else. They will have qualified in vain for a task they will not pursue and could be unprepared still for the job they will do.

Conflict generates a different kind of disturbance. This is a form of instability that is to be distinguished from competition. It is unfortunate that it has not always been distinguished. Dahrendorf, for instance, chooses to define *conflict* generically so as to include *competition*.[9] But it seems better to keep the term *conflict* for what has been identified as the zero-sum game: the situation where one party's gain is some advantage subtracted from the other. Conflict is the relationship that exists between two parties when this is the intention of it. This is not the case in competition. For there the parties are striving for a prize that neither possesses yet, and each tries to outmaneuver the other to win it. What one party finally gains the other forgoes, but it is not actually taken from him, for he never had it. If competition is conducted under rules that are accepted by all contenders, there is no reason why it should shade into conflict in any way. It seems that it only becomes the occasion for conflict if one party is not satisfied with the justice of the outcome and tries to diminish his opponent in retaliation. Conflict is essentially that kind of action: the attempt to seize an increment of power. However ill-advised or ill-fated it may in the end prove to be, its object is always the destruction of an opponent, his domination or diminution. For as long as the battle rages the outcome is in doubt and it is likely to be hurtful to one party or both. Armaments and the attack, repulsion and counterattack can also involve waste. Where the power balance allows it, however, conflict may

[9] R. Dahrendorf, *Class and Class Conflict in Industrial Society* (Stanford: Stanford University Press, 1963), pp. 133–36.

be obviated by a *bargain*. *Bargaining* is taking what one wants for an agreed price instead of seizing it directly.

I group *alienation* here with *competition* and *conflict*. I have suggested that it is a completely separate and distinct thing from *anomie*, with which it has sometimes been linked. For *alienation* describes a breach in social organization, not in culture, and represents the state of autonomy of individuals whose loyalty to the system has not been maintained. It is an extreme of disorganization in that it is a fairly complete atomization. And yet not totally. For what we call the "alienated" normally remain in the society as passengers. Although they drag their feet and make scant contribution, they continue to be a charge on the system. There is some point, then, in representing this position as lying beyond conflict. The alienated are distinguished from the active enemies of the system by the fact that they have no power to oppose it. "Would-be" enemies they very likely are, and, if organized, could become. But "playing it cool" is their only recourse for now.

Whatever the eventuality arising from grievance—competition, conflict, alienation—the basement beneath every social system is piled with inflammatory tinder. Justice is the thing that damps it, although it is essentially subjective justice—justice seen and felt to be sufficient ("fair enough") by those concerned. And what is accepted as sufficient today may appear in a different light tomorrow—even without the situation changing. This is the craving in the elementary social nature of man that has to be appeased by the institutions man makes if it is not to devour them. Homans, having explored this *subinstitutional* level of behavior, points out how men face a problem perennially of reconciling their institutions with it.[10] The *accommodation* and *assimilation* of Park and Burgess could be regarded as stages on the way to the reconciliation.[11] Unfortunately, as they defined them, these processes do not stand out very distinctly. I take it that accommodation is the process of giving in to superior odds, the "if you can't beat 'em join 'em" attitude. It only occurs, of course, if the weaker party believes he will advantage by surrender. Accommodation is made in particulars and by degrees. Assimilation occurs when the surrender has become more or less total and the party endorses the all-engulfing social order as legitimate.

It seems to be the ability to secure order through justice that earns legitimacy for any power in the end. Democrats should not let their ideology make them think democratic procedures are what secure legitimacy. These are simply precautions to limit abuse. Overrigidly adhered

[10] G. C. Homans, *Social Behavior: Its Elementary Forms* (New York: Harcourt, Brace & World, Inc., 1961), pp. 378–98.

[11] R. E. Park and E. W. Burgess, *Introduction to the Science of Sociology* (Chicago: The University of Chicago Press, 1924), pp. 663–784.

to, they can even obstruct legitimacy—as when an equal vote is exercised by persons unequally affected by an issue or unequally informed on it. It is not impossible for decisions made that way to tyrannize. It is much more likely that order secured by justice is what generates a willingness to identify with a system and assimilate, however the decisions are made. Are not Weber's three types of legitimation of power [12] simply different ways of securing this desideratum under different conditions? *Tradition* does it for the static society once its *modus operandi* is achieved. *Legislation* does it for the society that has constitutional procedures for implementing change. *Charismatic leadership* does it for the society that is in a crisis of order, there having been no constitutional anticipation of some contingency that has arisen. As conditions of stability, then, "sufficing" justice and order must be added to the indices of social normality. It is on this legitimation that enduring systems of social stratification rest.

Some people's misgivings about functionalism stem from a suspicion that the positive regard it pays to stability implies a condemnation of just revolt. But this is a misreading of functionalism's case; and it is unfortunate if, because of it, lovers of justice have failed to take functionalists for their friends. Actually, functionalism implies that a *system is deficient* in respect of stability if anyone under it withdraws support through being denied justice. It is, besides, an implication of our dialectical approach that the costs of competition, conflict, and alienation are not necessarily wasted. They can be profit-yielding investments if they are made the occasion of a sounder stability through increased order and justice. (It is not sociology's task to make an appraising judgment on this but a characterizing one, of course. Yet it is interesting that the appraising judgments of Marxism and orthodox Christianity, if I understand them correctly, are both in correspondence here with sociology's characterizing one and with one another. Do not both of them say that if authority is assumed without an acceptance of responsibility to promote justice and order, it is to be resisted and overthrown?)

Integration

Now we come to the third level of Figure II. This represents the internal challenge of the rationality requirement. For if, to cope with "present and foreseeable circumstances," a diversity of arrangements is made by the one set of individuals, the arrangements must be integrated among themselves. This third imperative is imposed on social organization, therefore, and is conspicuously evident whenever the system to be analyzed has more than one side to it. *Integration* has been used in the

12 M. Weber, *The Theory of Social and Economic Organization*, trans. A. M. Henderson and T. Parsons, ed. T. Parsons (New York: The Free Press of Glencoe, Inc., 1947), pp. 324–423.

phrase *social integration* as a synonym for *social cohesion* or *solidarity*—but I am making these synonymous with social organization itself. I prefer to keep *integration* for one component dimension of this more embracing concept. In doing so, I can capitalize on its more precise meaning. I will use it, therefore, for the internal orderliness of any *combination* of social arrangements. The enlistment of members' allegiance to the group, as will be apparent, I treat as an aspect of *stability*.

Just as a discourse needs to be coherent and consistent to be convincing, a social system of any complexity needs to be integrated to be productive. For just as a discourse draws separate facts together, such a social system is compounded of a number of sets of arrangements. Food production, say, as well as the maintenance of health and the taking of recreation, may all be undertaken by one set of people. These various activities must be so *deployed* that they do not interfere with one another, as they will if, for instance, they are all scheduled for one time. They will also interfere with one another if the product of one is an obstacle to the achievement of another—as when some food which is harmful to health is produced and used. The free proliferation of arrangements seems to be quite characteristic of social activities: they "just grow," like Topsy. Yet the compatibility of their ends has always ultimately to be faced by a group if they are not to leave themselves open to self-defeat. An everlasting review of activities in the social forum is therefore just as characteristic: they become due for *rationalization*. All questions of the compatibility of ends are really economic questions, in the most generic sense of that term. For these considerations are forced on us by scarcity—by how far the material will stretch. Included in "the material" in this case is that of which man himself is made. Being in a state of contradiction, for example, can be intellectually, emotionally, or morally insupportable for man because of the way he is made—just as it is impossible for a cake to be both actual and eaten because of the nature of cakes. This scarcity forces people to settle on some hierarchy of their preferences, so that they will know which to further when the ends compete with one another. It may force them further: They may have to settle whether any aims can be pursued for their own sake and without limit (and such aims alone I would call their *values*). Thus the very multiplicity of their deeds can lead men to a commitment to values, for the sake of setting their lives in order. Whereas under culture we consider the commitment the culture enjoins, under social organization we consider the commitment actually made.

Although all coordinating efforts contribute to social integration, legislation and adjudication can be two of its most deliberate expressions. The rationalization of work routines, social planning, commissions of inquiry—these are some others. But the sanctifying operations of religion probably provide the prototypical instance of integration. This is the group's radical approach to integration, in that it is not the object of religion to deny any normal activity, but to deny autonomy of aim to every activity. All activities, and the society itself, are recalled to the service of an overmastering end, and thereby integrated among themselves. Under culture we consider the symbolization that *defines* typical activities in such a way as to make them meaningful in relation to the whole of life. Here we consider the efforts taken to steer action by this chart.

Although the combining of *sets* of activities is what highlights the integration imperative, such combination enters into every division of labor, however minute. If two men do the same thing by throwing their weight against an obstacle, they have divided their labor rationally by each contributing a fraction of the work needed. If they do different things, one sowing the crop and the other reaping it, they have divided their labor rationally for the same reason. But if they push on opposite sides of the obstacle, or if one sows and the other plows directly after sowing, they have combined their efforts irrationally; for their separate efforts do not constitute a fraction of the work needed for the task. The integration of activities is essentially a matter of coupling them in a rational way so as to effect fruitful ends. Although we take it very much for granted in daily life, the need to work out a useful division of labor in all that we do shows that we are under constraint from an integration imperative continually. Some peoples are more notorious than others for their "muddling through," but there seems to be a certain inevitable fumbling, and subsequent improvement, in all cooperation. It is a crucial sociological question whether the improvement made on any occasion is sufficient to eliminate the initial confusion.

Satisfaction

It is because the demand for need-satisfaction through them is unrelenting that social arrangements must achieve adaptive change, stability, and integration. It is for this reason that judgments of function or dysfunction, normality or pathology, presuppose a whole catalogue of assumptions about human needs. It was said that part of our judgment that an operation is functional rests on our assumption that the product of the operation is needed by man. This must be one of the main reasons why functional thinking seems unsatisfactory to many people—for who shall say what the things are that man must have under all circumstances? And who shall so disentangle the inherited need from its cultural modification as to evelute the latter as a means of supplying the former? Yet, unsatisfactory though this admittedly seems, such assumptions must be made if sociological work is to have depth and significance. These assumptions form a backdrop of our own providing to all the empirical observations we make. But the backdrop is not itself nonempirical for all that. It has been woven from the cumulative experience of mankind, as we have each been able to absorb this. When we dealt with "needs" under culture, we were concerned with knowing whether a culture defines man's needs correctly in the values it enjoins. At this point, we bring in our direct judgment of what his needs are in order to say how successfully he acts to fulfil them. We can accept the best guidance psychology has to offer us on man's needs, but it seems that psychology will hardly take us far enough. Many of man's needs are functions of his situation.

We accept as human *needs* all those satisfactions that men have striven to repeat at many different times and places and by many different means. We assume that men need food, for example, because, under so many varied circumstances, we know they have acted as though they needed it. It is not for any different reason that we assume they need shelter, mutual protection, status, skilfulness, explanations of natural phenomena, and the consolations of religion. What any sociologist assumes here should hardly be that minimum range of needs to which all his colleagues will give ready assent, but that whole spectrum which his own vision has permitted him to see. It is precisely here that the social scientist is served by his explorations of the arts and humanities, as well as by the diversity of his experience and his range of sympathy and imagination. Perhaps it is by exceptional endowment here that the great sociologist is marked out. If he lends us his eyes for a time, we may devise instruments that will compensate other men for their partial blindness. And yet it is not the *sociological* problem to discover what man's needs are: we assume these from what is known. Our problem is to measure the satisfaction or deprivation of them by the social system in question and the impoverishment or enrichment effected by change.

chapter 9

The General Applicability
of the Model

It would show a complete misunderstanding of this book if the conceptual scheme in it were taken for anything other than a heuristic. Unless that is understood, there could simply be one more occasion for needless recriminations against "grand theory."

I have tried to suggest that exercises in the definition of analytical concepts need not be fruitless. But the value of such ventures depends on their place being understood. These definitions must be tested against experience, and possibly transformed, before they can be the terms of explanatory theory. While we are using them, our thinking never ceases to be in the interrogative mood. "Is not the world like this?" we are all the time asking. Equipped with such a scheme, we have a compass to guide our explorations, a map projection on which to draw a map. We have, in short, in the sense that I have suggested is most meaningful, a model. In the present case, it is a general model of the whole field of the discipline. Although it is almost certainly mistaken in particulars, this model does claim to have comprehensiveness. It lays down the cardinal dimensions of measurement for the social system and process *as such*. It gives the terms in which questions of sociological relevance may be asked. Yet to claim comprehensiveness for it is not to claim exhaustiveness. *All* the terms of sociology are not here, but there is *a place* here for all of them: it should be possible to fold any sociological term in. It should be locatable on this map projection and definable by the position it takes relative to others. Just as the concepts of culture and social organization have been separated into component strands, these can be separated into finer strands again. By that process of fission new concepts would be born.

If I have succeeded in any degree in giving a model of the social system and process *as such,* it should be applicable to any group regardless of scale. No doubt, difference in size introduces important differences of other kinds between groups. But this does not prevent the possibility of properties common to all. We may have to look hard to see things as the same thing, of course, when they show up in vastly varying magnitudes. Besides, we may have given the same things different everyday names, simply because of their difference in size. Yet we are not slow to see the sameness in a quarrel and a war, in a domineering partner and dictatorship, in getting our day sorted out and regional planning, in communicating a flash of inspiration and exercising charismatic leadership. It is possible, however, that we will experience difficulty in finding a term which is appropriate for groups of all sizes. What, for instance, is the small-group manifestation of *community?* We have to pause at this—yet not overlong. Fraternizing, camaraderie, conviviality, expressiveness of warmth and sympathy, striking a common chord, searching (maybe desperately) for a common interest, acquaintance, or experience—these are recognized aspects of small-group interaction that would make its "community" dimension. *Community* hardly seems an acceptable term for it, but *generalization* can accommodate it. Or, again, what is the manifestation in the organization of sacralization? This may appear quite unanswerable at first. Yet is it not all those definitions whereby the activities of separate departments are placed in subordination to the total effort and loyalty to the whole organization placed first?

We must acknowledge an important point, however, and the foregoing instances help to focus it sharply. Although we can find completely authentic parallels, in the small group and the organization, of the corresponding processes in the total society, the latter have certain unique qualities. Only in them are the phenomena generally allowed to have their "full expression," as we put it. For any social system that is a subsystem of another has boundary interchanges with the more inclusive system. These include understandings that are virtually protection agreements making it possible for the subsystem to restrict its scope. Thus the "community" in the neighborhood Christmas party does not have to be as broad, deep, and lasting as that by which a nation rears a civilization. Yet the former nests in the latter and draws strength from it. Nor does sacralization in the organization ordinarily lead to worship of the divine, whereas sacralization of the total life does. Here again, however, the former sacralization nests in the latter and leads to it by a succession of subordinations of parts to wholes. But we find it sufficient to use the term *institutionalization* for anything that stops short of the totality. With such qualifications granted, it is plausible to claim that the dimensions I have identified occur in social systems of any magnitude. It is only to be expected that in pointing them out one will seem to strain the use of language at times. Yet it takes fixed dimensions to *express* differences.

It would be a large undertaking indeed to illustrate all the system states and processes for systems at the four levels mentioned in Chapter 5. To do that in a systematic way might be a task for the future. All I shall do in this chapter is defend the plausibility of the claim to generality by offering illustrations. I shall take four illustrations from systems of face-to-face interaction, four from organizations, and two each from institutions and total societies. I shall only aim to show how each case bears on the model in certain particulars. My intention is to support the claim that all work that is sociological can be located here. Moreover, in this kind of exercise it will not concern us whether an author's terms have heuristic or empirical status.

As a first illustration of face-to-face interaction let us consider Bales' experimental work.[1] It is important for Bales that his actors start with "a problem." This means, in our language, that they are disoriented and in anomie. This is actually expressed in Bales' interaction categories 7, 8, and 9, when there is begging for orientation, opinions, and suggestions. (Bales' analytical categories are reproduced in Diagram 10.) The innovative response comes as orientation, opinions, and suggestions are offered (categories 4, 5, and 6). The "tasks" that Bales' subjects engage in can fairly be called culture-making, for their problem only finds a solution when they accept a set of directions as binding. Secularization is manifested in the piecemeal input of orientations. Giving opinions and suggestions constitutes more of the same kind of thing, in part. But it also includes the attempt to impose proportion and order on the information at hand (institutionalization and sacralization). It is Bales' view that the task that solves the initial problem generates a different problem, because carrying out a task is disruptive of solidarity. Categories 10, 11, and 12 express this disturbance: actions in these categories belong with the negative states and processes of the first two levels of our Figure II (p. 87). On the other hand, the expressions of solidarity and tension release of categories 1 and 2 belong with the recovery process of generalization, whereas decision through agreement belongs with the consolidation and legitimation of power, i.e., with recovery of stability.

What Bales and Strodtbeck have to say about phasing in the problem-

---

[1] R. F. Bales, *Interaction Process Analysis, A Method for the Study of Small Groups* (Cambridge, Mass.: Addison-Wesley Publishing Co., Inc., 1951). Data summarized by permission of the author.

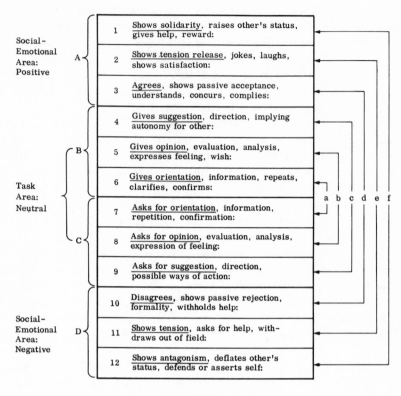

KEY

a   Problems of Communication
b   Problems of Evaluation
c   Problems of Control
d   Problems of Decision
e   Problems of Tension Reduction
f   Problems of Reintegration

A   Positive Reactions
B   Attempted Answers
C   Questions
D   Negative Reactions

Diagram 10

solving process also fits our scheme.[2] Expressions of concern with orientation are found to decline. This suggests that information can become
sufficiently plentiful in time (*norm sufficiency*). But evaluation, for the
sake of putting information in order, rises and remains fairly high
throughout (*institutionalization*). Concern with control, for the sake of
carrying the endorsed norms into effect, increases continuously (*stability*).

[2] R. F. Bales and F. L. Strodtbeck, "Phases in Group Problem Solving," *Journal
of Abnormal and Social Psychology*, **46** (1951), 485–95.

The negative social-emotional reactions increase all the time as the effort of all this takes its toll (*maladaptation* and *instability*). But there is also a final peak for positive social-emotional reactions, when the group commits itself by general agreement to the adaptations required of it (*adaptive change* and *stability*).

Next let us look for evidences of our model in Homans' *Social Behavior*.[3] Homans draws on a diversity of small-group studies in this book, but the controlling effects of rewards and penalties is strictly its theme. One main informing idea in it is that cooperation is stabilized by a just distribution of rewards, and that the parties to any relationship have it in their power to reward one another by their deeds. This locates Homans' treatise on the second level of Figure II. A typical finding he reports has to do with the way in which competition can become the occasion for conflict: if people who are in competition are also in a position to deprive one another of rewards which they have come to consider their due. Another typical finding is his conclusion that status congruence is the condition of distributive justice and social certitude alike. (*Status congruence* is where all the kinds of currency in which one is rewarded for the one performance have the same ranking.) Men consider the attainment of this state a particularly important reward, in Homans' view. A set of actors so rewarded constitutes a settled group. Finally, it will be apparent, as well as involving the second level of our Figure II, Homans' study involves the fourth. For he is convinced of the necessity of assuming that men are bent on satisfaction in all their encounters.

Now let us consider the matters Goffman handles in the two studies published under the title, *Encounters*,[4] taking the second one first. Goffman's delineation of the phenomenon he calls *"role distance"* falls on the second level of Figure I (p. 86). For it is the process of institutionalization that is so engaging to him, as this is observable in detail in interaction. He draws our attention to something that is often missed when role behavior is reported on: the fact that people sometimes deliberately suspend the role they are playing to express aspects of roles they play at other times. Thus the individual, to use Goffman's words, "frees himself from one group, not to be free, but because there is another hold on him."[5] Goffman shows that the practice is culturally regulated and occurs for good reason, i.e., it is functional. Wider claims can be acknowledged and fulfilled, over and above those demanding one's imme-

[3] G. C. Homans, *Social Behavior: Its Elementary Forms* (New York: Harcourt, Brace & World, Inc., 1961).

[4] E. Goffman, *Encounters: Two Studies in the Sociology of Interaction* (Indianapolis: The Bobbs-Merrill Co., Inc., 1961).

[5] *Ibid.*, p. 139. © 1961 by The Bobbs-Merrill Co., Inc. Reprinted by permission of the publisher.

diate attention. Thus a surgeon at work will "modulate his own demands and his own expectations of what is due to him" *as a surgeon* in order to fulfil what is needed from him *as a leader* of the surgery team.[6] Or if the intern punctuates his performance with levity—expressing, say, a mock physical attraction to the nurse—it is to remind everyone that his life includes other less demeaning roles than this, roles such as "the male." Now here is a transparent expression of both the proportioning and perpetuation of activity in institutionalization. It is an acknowledgment that our actions are legitimated by inclusion in coherent wholes that unfold through time, and that there are multiple wholes of this kind in our whole life.

The study that appears first in *Encounters,* "Fun in Games," has the same theme, for all its apparent difference. For it is Goffman's point that fun may be realized or missed when games are played. It is a kind of exhilaration or euphoria that comes through drawing an envelope or membrane around the gaming encounter: this creates a self-contained or meaningful world for the participants. This is done by establishing a whole pattern of rules of admissible conduct that prescribe, among other things, the proper degree of involvement for players. If everyone adheres to these rules, it is possible for the person to be wholly engrossed and surrender himself to a vivid sense of mastering *reality*. (This is what fun *is*.) Goffman considers the game to be only one case of such meaning-making activity, and I have suggested that this is what institutionalization is and that it finds its ultimate expression in sacralization. In play, the process is given a fictional expression in pretending—in art it is given a fictional expression in design. People can find "delight" in art and "fun" in games because they are the sort of creatures that can find "service" in institutions and "blessing" in religion. These are not the same things, by any means, but they are the same *kinds* of things. Their achievement rests on the same *kinds* of conditions. It is a precarious prize always, but it is a prize that is taken when a set of persons surrender to rules that immerse them in a system where they "lose themselves."

Some of Schelling's observations on the strategy of conflict can be examined next.[7] These belong to the second level of Figure II, of course. I introduce them in further illustration of our model on the small-scale, face-to-face level, yet it is Schelling's understanding that the transactions he analyzes can be reproduced on all levels of scale, whether it be of persons or of nations. Let us take his essay on bargaining. Schelling apparently accepts bargaining as an attempt to obviate or limit conflict, and in this essay he explores the distributional aspect of it: "the situations in

---

[6] *Ibid.,* p. 121.

[7] T. C. Schelling, *The Strategy of Conflict* (Cambridge, Mass.: Harvard University Press, 1963).

which a better bargain for one means less for the other." [8] He represents
the situation in this way:

> There is some range of alternative outcomes in which any point
> is better for both sides than no agreement at all. To insist on any
> such point is pure bargaining, since one always *would* take less
> rather than reach no agreement at all, and since one always *can*
> recede if retreat proves necessary to agreement.[9]

Schelling shows that bargaining is a way of binding oneself at a point
where one anxiously hopes the other party will concede to one's demand—
rather than bring the relationship to an end in stalemate. As the stronger
party wants some cooperation from the weaker, he cannot exploit his
power advantage to directly diminish the weaker. What his power advantage does enable him to do is strike the terms of a bargain, for he must
pay for the cooperation he seeks. As bargaining is a resolution or termina-
tion of conflict, it involves the recovery as much as the disturbance of
Level II. By whatever means he does it, one party is able to persuade the
second that his power advantage is such that they have reached the point
where the second must "take it or leave it." If the second agrees to take it
and not leave it, a stabilization is reached. There is legitimation, by mutual acceptance, of a distribution of gains.

As a first illustration of the applicability of the schema to social
systems at the managerial level, let us consider McCleery's report, *Policy
Change in Prison Management*.[10] This is an account of revolution in the
organization. In it, the goal of *treatment* comes to challenge *custody* as
the dominant goal of a prison. A liberal group that favored treatment
took over from the old guard that had secured its authority by a tight
control on communication. McCleery makes much of the part that can be
played by communication. He says that a pattern of communication can
serve as a functional equivalent for force in maintaining or subverting
authority. It might, of course, be said that *control* over communication is
in fact a form of coercion rather than a functional equivalent for it. But,
whichever way it is viewed, it seems this liberal group prised the traditional situation open by a habit of open communication. These men,
recently appointed, bypassed the custodial force and turned to one another and to the newly appointed Warden for definitions. They found
the Warden rankling under the limits placed on his discretion by the
custodial control of communication, they then made a policy caucus

---

8 *Ibid.*, p. 21. Reprinted by permission of the publisher.
9 *Ibid.*, p. 22.
10 R. H. McCleery, "Policy Change in Prison Management," in *Complex Organizations, A Sociological Reader,* ed. A. Etzioni (New York: Holt, Rinehart & Winston, Inc.,
1962), pp. 376–400.

around him. By securing information for themselves they upset the custodians' method of controlling decision by controlling the information on which it is based. They produced a diagram of the formal organization and, in it, placed treatment and industry on a level with the guard force. They constituted themselves into a policy committee and produced a Policy and Philosophy Manual. The Manual defined rehabilitation, through treatment and industry, as the primary institutional goal and affirmed the democratic approach to management. The old guard put up resistance to this encroachment, but in the end it proved in vain. Now this episode in the life of a prison is located on the second level of Figure II. It involves conflict, instability, and the recovery of a new stability. Also, as I have pointed out in Chapter 8, those are processes that entail the opening and closing of communication channels.

Blau's analysis of the dynamics of bureaucracy supplies another example at the managerial level.[11] It nests neatly in the schema on the first level of both Figure I and II. His thesis is that changes in routine are constantly forced on bureaucratic organizations. Such adjustments are effected by the implementation of innovations. But innovations are themselves disorienting and necessitate further adjustments. Thus Blau captures the spiraling nature of the process in the same way as my schema tries to do. For instance, the employment agency under study started keeping statistical records in order to improve placement operations. But this engendered competitiveness in its officers, which interfered with both general productivity and the service given to handicapped clients. In response to these two organizational needs, further innovations developed. Special interviewers for handicapped clients assumed duties that placed other interviewers under an obligation also to help find jobs for the handicapped. In addition, one group of the regular interviewers devised methods for discouraging competitive tendencies—which raised their production again.

Blau not only draws attention to a cultural aspect in norm-making, he comments on what he calls the "conditions" for that adjustment. This moves the discussion across to generalization. He says it is only possible for adaptive changes to be effected in organizations if certain cushioning conditions obtain—exactly the kinds of thing I have grouped under *generalization*. The actors have to be rendered plastic by these conditions in order to bend. Blau therefore stresses a community factor in three separate expressions: a minimum of employment security, a lack of basic conflict between work group and management, and established work groups that command the allegiance of the members. He stresses an ideological factor as well in the employee's commitment to a professional

11 P. M. Blau, *The Dynamics of Bureaucracy, A Study of Interpersonal Relations in Two Government Agencies* (Chicago: The University of Chicago Press, 1955).

orientation. Conditions like these allow adaptive changes to go forward.

Next consider Goffman's account of those organizations he calls *"total institutions."* [12] Here his attention rests on the same kind of thing that he analyzes under role distance and fun in games. Goffman is the sociologist *sans doute,* and the making of social institutions by enveloping practices in a context is what entrances him. Organizations like hospitals, prisons, barracks, and convents he calls "total institutions" for the reason that they make themselves responsible for the inmates' total life. Such institutions create a world of their own, but they do so by exploiting their inmates' prior socialization to a home world beyond. Total institutions do not, he says, look for cultural victory.

> They create and sustain a particular kind of tension between the home world and the institutional world and use this persistent tension as strategic leverage in the management of men.[13]

By processes of mortification, they strip the inmate of his accustomed supports. They then hold out to him as privileges certain rewards which in the home world would be regarded as very minor or taken for granted. On the outside, for instance, he had unthinking autonomy in deciding how much sugar and milk he wanted in his coffee, if any, or when he might smoke. Inside, these things can be held up to him as rewards for conformity. The processes Goffman is tracing also pass into the third level of Figure I. For the problem confronting total institutions is to effect a drastic unification out of plural materials, the inmates having come from diverse backgrounds. Also, because it has to mount routines that provide for the inmates' total life, the total institution must have detailed and all-encompassing conformity. This is why it first reduces the inmates to identical atoms. Then it secures their devotion to itself by rewarding them with tokens of that larger life in which they had status, dignity, and freedom.

Our final illustration at this level is from Wilensky's study of trade unions.[14] In 1956, Wilensky sought to discover whether the trade union had the characteristics Weber ascribed to bureaucracy. He concluded from a case study that this was scarcely yet the case, though on the way. He gave us a picture, rather, of anomie. And recovery was being made from it by a combination of innovation and generalization. His study was mainly located, then, on the first level of both Figures. Wilensky dem-

12 E. Goffman, "On the Characteristics of Total Institutions: The Inmate World," in D. R. Cressey, ed., *The Prison: Studies in Institutional Organization and Change* (New York: Holt, Rinehart & Winston, Inc., 1961).

13 *Ibid.,* p. 23.

14 H. L. Wilensky, *Intellectuals in Labor Unions* (New York: The Free Press of Glencoe, Inc., 1956).

onstrated that a minute division of labor and a clear-cut hierarchy of authority were being forced on trade union organization by the exigencies of their growth. Meanwhile, however, and even as the formalization proceeds, there is an avid exploitation of informal channels of communication and influence for getting things done. There is, for instance, the practice of influencing the boss by planting your ideas with a third person who has access to him, or the practice of using the female secretarial contingent at headquarters for grapevine communication. It is as though an enhanced reliance on this personalist way of proceeding has flowered simultaneously with the determination to supplant it by the impersonal bureaucratic method of procedure by rule. Here, I suggest, we see the cushioning by generalization of the strain of rational innovation.

We turn now to the two illustrations from institutions. One that I have chosen is Dore's account of education in Tokugawa Japan.[15] Startlingly reminiscent of the way in which Weber traces the rise of capitalism in Europe to the rationalism of the Protestant conscience, Dore traces Japan's smooth and rapid transition from feudalism to industrialism to the rationalism of the Confucian ethic, as this was inculcated in the schools of the Tokugawa period. The samurai of feudal Japan lost their traditional prosperity and leadership in this period. They had hereditary status as a support force for the Shogun in the unification of the country, but wealth was increasingly generated by the merchant class, whereas the samurai's income came from a tax on agriculture. There was consequently widespread demoralization among them. It was hoped that by ethical instruction they would be held to their traditional responsibilities, but as the social organization was itself changing, this could not be realized. Nevertheless, there was a universalism in the Tokugawa Confucianism they absorbed in the schools that enabled them to reapply the *principles* of responsibility to radically changed circumstances. The very thing that might appear to make this kind of education redundant in a static society made it highly relevant to a changing one. For it was explicitly nonutilitarian, designed to make good men and, very largely, that meant showing the respect and responsibility due from one's status to the holders of other statuses. Confucianism was like a sociology in itself, and the method of imparting it by a study of history and of the Chinese classics gave the student a social and political awareness. Furthermore, the very formality of these studies, which might appear to rob them of realism, somehow disengaged the student from too great an attachment to any present reality, so that political activity became like a game. Military activity shared the same flavor; to find exhilaration in military expansion was all one with finding it in industrial expansion. That it should

[15] R. P. Dore, *Education in Tokugawa Japan* (London: Routledge & Kegan Paul, Ltd., 1965).

be for the glory of the nation and not the person was already determined by the citizens' Confucianism. For this insisted that service to the collectivity should override the pursuit of personal achievement or distinction. It also appears to be significant that Japanese modernization, different from that of Europe, was largely a matter of borrowing innovations that had been tried elsewhere. For this, too, their Confucianism had made the Japanese ready, for it was a very pervasive theme that one should be humbly receptive to light and respectful to the bearer of it.

The problems explored in Dore's study are located on the first level of the two Figures. There is anomie with the breakdown of the feudal economy and the eclipse of the samurai's leadership role. This is met by a variety of innovations: the merchandising economy and massive industrialization at length; a widening of the definition of eligibility for education, to extend the training in both literacy and the classics to more citizens; a stretching of the curriculum to include Western science and technology; and a new conception of leadership for the one-time samurai, as economic, political, and military activists. Of particular interest is the illustration the study affords of generalization in response to maladaptation. The recourse was to education in an ideology, which set out universal principles of social obligation. In places Dore seems to be bothered by a feeling that these obligations are defined particularistically in Confucianism—father and son, master and subordinate, and so on. Yet we see universalism too. It is defining obligations in terms of standard positions, irrespective of the particular ties, interests, or attractions of their occupants. If Dore's thesis is correct, it was adherence to universal precepts of duty such as these that made Japanese society elastic enough to industrialize rapidly. (He suggests that the record of the citizenry was far from unsullied but was good enough to bear fruit.) New society though nineteenth-century Japan might be, it had the primitive, perennial feature of the mutual dependence of weak and strong parts—as Confucius would have expected.

The second study of an institution is Berkes' account of the emergence of a modern state in Turkey.[16] The Ottoman-Turkish religious society that dated from the end of the fourteenth century had reached complete disorder by the end of the eighteenth. Change was due and there were many doors open toward the West through which technological and educational innovations entered. But Berkes shows that a lasting transformation of the society demanded that technical innovations have the backing of institutional reorganization, especially in government and the economy. Furthermore, institutional reorganization could only be effected when there was consolidation of a new Turkish community based

16 N. Berkes, *The Development of Secularism in Turkey* (Montreal: McGill University Press, 1964).

on nationality, to take the place of the Ottoman, Islamic community that had sponsored the traditional order. In actual fact, these desiderata of change appeared in reverse order from that required: first appeared the innovations, then the institutional reorganization, and, last of all, the national community. But each waited upon the coming of its successor: until that occurred its lease of life was tentative and wavering.

Turkey's first response to feudal breakdown was to appropriate the advantages of Western technology through government reforms in education. But simultaneous with progress in these was a growing vacuum within the indigenous economy and government. Yet, by the time attempts to repair these institutions had made some headway, the Islamic, Ottoman Empire was collapsing and there seemed to be no community of people to make the institutions their own. The revolution of 1908, however, had the effect of creating a national community that rallied in support of the regime that followed. Although the revolution was the work of a small band in the Society of Union and Progress, immediately as it was accomplished hundreds of new branches of the Society formed spontaneously, one in almost every town. Thus the Society became the basis of an emergent Turkish nation. The artisans and merchants of the towns were its main recruits, and it was in order to secure their interests that the new government was eventually needed. Government reform had been from above and, until that time, had lacked any community sponsorship. In all of this we observe innovation, in the recovery from anomie. But we also observe generalization in the emergence of a new community, in the recovery from maladaptation.

It is chiefly because of the way in which it documents the process of secularization that Berkes' book is of interest, however. It traces the steps by which a state divested of religious authority emerged. It shows the state becoming a rationally differentiated and isolated cultural item, separate from the religion with which it had been traditionally fused. For traditionally, the Ottoman Sultanate, the temporal power of the empire, was merged with the Caliphate, the spiritual headship of Islam. In addition, the body of academicians known as the Ulema were charged with seeing that the ruler's legislation, administration, and justice were in accordance with the Seriat, the sacred law of Islam. All of this made for an emphasis on traditional order, as distinct from change and reform. The thin end of the wedge that split the monolith, in Berkes' view, was a trend to democratization set in motion early in the nineteenth century by Mahmud II—almost, as it were, by stealth. He generated a new sphere of law-making outside the will of the Sultan-Caliph and outside the Seriat, and introduced a new notion of justice. In its medieval definition, justice consisted of reserving for each one what was due to him according to his status; the new view consisted of making everyone equal before the law. The new view also implied a source of legislation other than God and the sovereign: it was ultimately to be identified as "the people." As a consequence, the Ulema were silenced outside their allotted sphere, and there was much debate over what their sphere was. In time, separate codes were promulgated covering the responsibility of government officials and judges, commerce, penal law, and civil law. Mahmud also created a new center of government in the Porte, which became ascendent over the court. He created ministers to departments of government having differentiated functions: ultimately these included internal, external, financial, educational, commercial, agricultural, and industrial affairs.

Yet these and other secular changes somehow failed to make sense to many of the Turks, and there were constant waves of reaction. Patently, it was because they were not embedded in a total context of economic and political institutions that would make them meaningful and legitimate. The same situation was exemplified in the constitutional movement. A constitution for Turkey was what the Society of Young Ottomans wanted, and Turkey duly got its constitution. Then the absolutist Abdul-Hamid meticulously observed it while proroguing the Assembly for over thirty years. It took the revolution of 1908, the emergence of a Turkish nation from the ashes of the Ottoman Empire, and Mustafa Kemal's charismatic leadership thereafter to establish a democratic government that made all these practices meaningful. Simultaneously, a great deal of traditional practice became meaningless. Even though it took place under a cloud of stultified verbal protest, it was then possible to have acts passed abolishing both the Sultanate and Caliphate. Islam was bruised by all this but not broken. It emerged modernized and, although Berkes does not pursue its course, it will doubtless be seeking a more spiritual way to give religious sanction to a separated state.

It remains to illustrate the model in two studies of total societies. For this I have chosen one study of a primitive society and one of a complex one: Turnbull's *The Forest People* and Williams' *American Society*.[17] In *The Forest People*, Turnbull gives an anthropologist's account of the life of the Pygmies of the Congo. It is, of course, characteristic of anthropologists to show a people setting the stage for a meaningful total life by building a unified culture. In demonstrating this for the Pygmies, Turnbull repeatedly comes back to two sources of threat to the meaningfulness of their life. There are, first of all, internal shocks like death, illness, and famine. These are dealt with by transvaluation. The natural event is placed in a supernatural context until faith in the goodness of the presence that sustains them is revived, and this presence is their whole nur-

[17] C. M. Turnbull, *The Forest People* (New York: Simon & Schuster, Inc., 1961). R. M. Williams, Jr., *American Society, A Sociological Interpretation*, 3rd ed. (New York: Alfred A. Knopf, Inc., 1966).

turant universe, the Forest itself. Here we observe sacralization plainly. After crises, the Pygmies sing to the Forest in songs of ravishing beauty and in festivals that may continue every day for months—in order to make it happy again. This gives them assurance that whatever had to be is good. On certain occasions, also, the festivals may bring them to the source of their own individual and collective life and show them to be privileged vessels of it in the sexual act. For there are times when, during the singing, dancers swirl into the fire and are unable to kick it out: it comes up strong again, symbolizing the virility of men. Turnbull's study touches the fourth level of our schema, the level concerned with satisfaction. He is much impressed by the happiness the Pygmies achieve through this realization of meaning.

The other threat to the meaningfulness of the Pygmies' life comes with cultural pluralism through outside contacts. Contact with neighboring Negroes, with missionaries, and with government officers are all experienced, although it is the first that appears to loom largest. Turnbull is at pains to detail the Pygmies' exact response in these situations, for he is convinced that the Pygmies make very little concession to anything outside their Forest life. Cultural pluralism is intolerable to them, and whatever is not of the Forest they simply reject. If circumstance compels them to conform to any patterns that do not take their sanction from the Forest, they do so expediently, putting on a show. This is most obviously the case in their participation in the Negro initiation rites for boys. Negroes will not recognize even Pygmies as having adult status unless they undergo the Negro initiation, so for this reason the Pygmies have their sons submit to it. They go through with it not to enter into it but for the sake of what is contingent on it. A similar attitude of mind is expressed when the Pygmies, reared as hunters and gatherers, accept beans from the government officer in order to start plantations of their own— then cook the beans for lunch. That it is not impossible—though difficult —to unlock a cultural closure, given a common term for the key, is also illustrated. The anthropologist takes one of the Pygmies right out of his accustomed environment. We see then that even a new landscape is like a torment to the Pygmy, so difficult is it to accept. But apparently its power has sufficient affinity with the Forest's for him to assimilate them at last. En route he has exchanged conversation with a Catholic Father, who is an enlightened teacher indeed, it appears. The Pygmy is finally seized by the glory of the landscape and concedes that what the Father said was right—this God and the God in the Forest must be the same.

Williams' study attempts the Herculean feat of accounting for American society as a whole. As could only be expected, he has to be satisfied with considerably less than he wished for, especially in confining himself to a static view. But he does succeed in showing how differentiated from one another American institutions are, each in a way a world in itself, and that each one comprises an intricate network of norms. That each sphere of life generates some autonomy for itself is not lessened by the fact that they can impinge on one another. For instance, although government undertakes to provide facilities, procedures, and regulations for adjusting management-labor disputes, this very fact demonstrates that the economy has an autonomy that constrains the government to act just as much as it shows that the government exercises autonomy.

Of some special interest to us are Williams' comments on the patterned evasion of institutional norms. He draws attention to the way an honored social institution can set a standard that is not exactly matched to the modest needs of human nature, so that ways have to be found around it—what I have called *cultural duplicity* develops. One illustration is found in the subversion of the merit system of appointment and promotion in American governments, another in the perversion of justice through rigged or incompetent juries, another in political corruption when business interests buy protection or privilege and criminals buy immunity, another in racial discrimination when this is practiced by people pledged to equality. Williams suggests that evasions like these must be recognized, for they point to needs that the institution has failed to reckon with. They are like a commentary on, or dialogue with, the institution. Do they, then, presage change? Possibly their occurrence means that the institution should have been more balanced or discriminating in itself, or more detailed and precise.

The chief interest to us in Williams' book, however, is his attempt in the concluding chapter to account for the stability of American society. In view of its great size and complexity and the diversity of interests and cultural origins of its population, its stability might indeed seem surprising. Williams invokes a combination of five factors to explain it. First, vast numbers of individuals expect some gain through keeping the system going, even though the gain to each one may be very different. America has perhaps been exceptionally fortunate in that so many of its citizens have experienced an increasing prosperity, so many have a stake in the nation's welfare. Secondly, there has been an elaboration of techniques of coordination and integration. Thirdly, there have been external pressures generated by actual or potential enemies, that have welded the people into a community in the defense of their opportunities. Fourthly, there are in any case commonly held values among Americans, notwithstanding their divergent interests. And, finally, the very diversity of the memberships available to individuals contributes to a national unity. For, insofar as each person has multiple pulls on his allegiance they tend, so to speak, to cancel out. As a result, the citizenry cannot be divided easily into opposing camps. Williams uses *stability* in a less precise sense than mine, of course. His five factors, taken in order, exemplify what I would class as stability, integration, community, sacralization, and integration again.

Our review of studies is now complete. Even if, like Molière's gentleman, they spoke prose without knowing it, the authors of them were speaking to the fundamental questions of sociology—or so I would claim. Workers of the future will need their steady eye. But, in addition, it seems desirable that they *position* their contributions more deliberately than most workers of the past have been able to do, by reference to the general field. If they can show on which of the universal system states and processes their observations bear, it will aid the consolidation of a science.

Of course there is little yet, in the studies we have considered, of the quantitative precision I am demanding. But this could come with future work as conviction about the dimensions of measurement stabilizes. In the concluding chapter I make some comments on this measurement challenge. If anyone finds this book persuasive and cares to build on it, research in the style indicated in that chapter will do more than anything else to help. But there is an impetus in this book for further work in four distinct directions, of which empirical measurement is only one. Other scholars, with other abilities and tastes, might also take a point of departure from what is set forth here. It would be possible to use the present conceptual scheme, precisely in a way that this chapter illustrates, to systematically consolidate all existing knowledge in the field. That would make a second task. A third task would be for students of the history of ideas to trace the whole ancestry of the concepts which I have claimed to be cardinal for sociological analysis. A fourth task would be virtually to do again what I have done in Chapters 7 and 8. The exercise in definition undertaken there can be progressively refined of course.

There is, finally, another direction of inquiry leading out from here, although it is one that passes beyond the bounds of sociology. I have tried to find terms of great generality for a conceptual scheme for sociology. With increasing generality one's terms tend to become isomorphic with the terms used in other fields of study. Structure, function, process, and system clearly have universality. Adaptation, stability, integration, and satisfaction are scarcely any less universal. Those four terms, used in reference to social organization, are given analogues in my scheme for culture, and it is possible that they would have analogues in other fields of study besides. There is probably more sentiment than sense in a great deal of the talk about interdisciplinary study. But a line of thought that promises to be fruitful is the one of applying the same analytical concepts across a number of disciplines. I would hope to have made sociology more amenable to this kind of companionship with other sciences. Both in defending its distinctiveness and in expounding its most general dimensions, I hope I have built a good fence for sociology that will serve to make it a good neighbor.

chapter 10

The Implication
for Research

I have tried to drive home certain fundamentals, hoping thereby to revive the fading vision of a general sociology. Explanatory theory wants measured variations to explain. These have to be variations in the properties of social systems if the theory is to be sociological. It is important that we think quantitatively, but it is equally important that we know how to frame a question of sociological science. We should ask what variations in social systems occur together. Is improved adaptation associated with either a loss in stability or a gain? Is innovation associated with either cultural pluralization or cultural unification? Is legitimation associated with either greater or less integration? Is secularization associated with either adaptation or maladaptation? This is the form of the questions to be raised. And if the results of this research enterprise are to be cumulative, studies will need to be framed in these general and fixed terms. Studies must be shaken free from the particularities of time and space and the domination of practical concerns.

More exacting than any of this is the matter of making measurements of a material as dialectical as I have suggested society is. Things can be getting better and worse together. In fact, it is almost safe to assume they will be, since the social engine never does stand still. Anytime we turn our gaze on a group it will be poised, in multiple respects, between positive and negative forces. We have therefore to specify its condition by taking out a kind of balance for each dimension. Because this measurement is the same as evaluation, that is only what would be expected, for when making evaluation we weigh the pros and cons.

It seems, though, that this requires us to make some decisions about a scale. For instance, where is zero? This and the other questions do not have to be answered categorically and once for all here. But a suggestion can be made. Each positive state constitutes a kind of perfect possibility, so the most direct procedure might be to measure declensions from them. What degree of instability exists? What degree of meaninglessness? What degree of malintegration? What degree of deprivation?—and so on. This would be analogous to measuring the temperature of a body by its deviation from the freezing point of water. If we choose to think about the matter in this way, we have then to decide on units. How shall we measure an increment of each of these properties?

There is also the question of measuring the evolutionary advancement of a group, the question of distinguishing, say, between stability$_1$, where the group is comparatively simple and undifferentiated, and stability$_2$, where it is comparatively complex and differentiated. It may be equally stable at both points, but in the second instance it has achieved this state by mastering a greater challenge. For this we need comparative measures of internal differentiation.

Furthermore, insofar as we want to specify processes, as distinct from states, we will be measuring rates of change. Rationalization, as a process, is a rate of change in malintegration, innovation a rate of change in anomie. Differentiation, too, can have its rate of change. And these rates themselves can increase or decrease in pace: there can be a rate of change of a rate of change. Unification or generalization may slacken or accelerate in their progress, perhaps with an effect on the rate of other processes. The social processes, then, have the features of derivatives like velocity and acceleration.

One need not say that asking for a solution to all these problems is asking a lot. But if aspiring sociologists want a challenging career, why should they not find the challenge in this?

Index

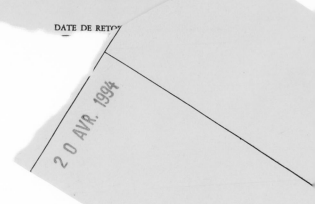